Loving Through Bars

Children with Parents in Prison

Cynthia Martone

Loving Through Bars

Children with Parents in Prison

Cynthia Martone

SANTA
MONICA
PRESS

Published by:
Santa Monica Press LLC
P.O. Box 1076
Santa Monica, CA 90406-1076
1-800-784-9553
www.santamonicapress.com
books@santamonicapress.com

Printed in the United States

Santa Monica Press books are available at special quantity discounts when purchased in bulk by corporations, organizations, or groups. Please call our Special Sales department at 1-800-784-9553.

Library of Congress Cataloging-in-Publication Data

Martone, Cynthia, 1956–
  Loving through bars : children with parents in prison / by Cynthia Martone.
      p. cm.
  Includes bibliographical references.
  ISBN 1-891661-48-5
  1. Children of prisoners—United States. 2. Prisoners—United States—Family relationships. I. Title.
  HV8886.U5M366 2005
  362.82'95'0973—dc22

                                                                        2004027524

Cover photo by Rubberball Productions/Mark Andersen/Getty Images. The child in the photograph is a model and is being used for illustrative purposes only.

Author photograph courtesy of William Pohl and the photography students of Villa Maria Academy, Erie, Pennsylvania.

Cover and interior design by Lynda "Cool Dog" Jakovich.

Contents

Acknowledgments

A very special thank you to my mother, Mary Ida Martone, for her endless hours of editing this work.

For members of my family who have supported me: Rita, Scott, and Haley Heitzenrater, Edward Martone and Joseph and Dianne Martone.

Danielle Heitzenrater for her transcribing and computer editing support.

The following Rochester City Police Officers: Nicole Cookinham, Mark Mariano, Bryan Trombley, Dave Williams and Flamur Zenelovic.

Sergeant Alfred DeRosa, Monroe County Sheriffs Office.

Bolgen Vargas a guidance counselor who is an exemplar in his field.

John Tando, East Rochester Police for opening doors to the prison world.

Kelly Semple for her untiring support on all levels.

Dr. Rufino Pabico for enlightening me to the wisdom of the ages.

Patricia Dottore, a true friend who has listened to and supported me unconditionally.

Robert Miller of Cephas House for opening my eyes to the other side of the story.

Norma Amendola for her hours of transcription.

Steve Robbins for his technical and personal support of the work.

Attorney Peter Durant for his legal advice and guidance.

Joann Lester for her active support of the Loving Through Bars non-profit organization.

Jackie Rubenstein for helping me to write an incredible query and for her guidance.

My publisher, Jeffrey Goldman—I'm grateful to destiny for assuring our paths crossed. Thank you for believing in me, and the need for the work.

Attorney William H. Burke for support in the Loving Through Bars non-profit organization.

David Heitzenrater for opening doors and supporting the non-profit and me.

The photograph of me is courtesy of William Pohl and the photography students of Villa Maria Academy, Erie, Pennsylvania.

Cynthia Martone
January 2005

This book is dedicated to my children,
Lisa and Brian, the driving force
behind their mother.

Author's Note

According to the wishes of the children and parents interviewed for this book, no person has been identified by his or her real name or actual physical characteristics. The dialogue is constructed from notes and taped interviews. Any apparent inconsistencies in statements made by those interviewed are reflections of the individuals who spoke them.

Introduction

I used to write poetry
But haven't lately
Who would I show it to…?
About him in prison
About shame, About waiting
About loving someone
Anyway
—*Anonymous*

More than 2.3 million children in the United States have a parent in prison. These children are innocent victims, their lives filled with instability and uncertainty and damaged by stigma and shame. Children with an incarcerated parent comprise a neglected segment of our society lost in a vicious cycle that often leads to future criminality and deviant social behavior. They are child prisoners—children who must learn to understand living and loving through bars.

For me, the discovery began when I learned of the circumstances surrounding two students—a second-grade girl and her first-grade brother. When I realized the children were going to be spending the weekend with their incarcerated father at the infamous Attica State Prison, and I read a letter in their file from their father asking that he be allowed to participate in his children's education, I found myself determined to understand all aspects of the situation: what the children would experience, what their father was trying to accomplish, how the nature of their relationship had been affected by the incarceration of the father. . . .

The very word "prison" evokes a sense of doom, of a dark pit for the soul. Prisons are bleak places, but to children with someone they love behind those bars, the surroundings become secondary to the stolen moments of being loved—of loving—that can occur within prison walls. For the sake of these children, I chose to enter the prison world through their eyes. Thus began my journey into thoughts, feelings, and experiences I had never encountered. It was a decision that changed my life.

There is a devastating effect on children whose parents do not, for whatever reason, fulfill their roles. These children have been deprived of the most important factor to their growth and development: parental love. Parental love begins with parental presence. In *Between Parents and Child,* Dr. Haim G. Ginnott underscores the fact that "a child's greatest fear is of being unloved and abandoned by his parents." And this same belief is echoed and immortalized by John Steinbeck in his novel, *East of Eden:* "The greatest terror a child can have is that he is not loved, and rejection is the hell he fears . . . And with rejection comes anger, and with anger some kind of crime in revenge."

In my role as a school principal, I have learned of homeless children, HIV positive children, and children abandoned by parents who are so self-absorbed that the only alternative for their children is a foster home. And yet I did not become aware of the issue of children who have a parent in prison until relatively late in my career in education. These children are most certainly a neglected segment of our society, and the impact on all of our lives cannot be underestimated. We can no longer ignore them.

Children do not comprehend the mechanism and the principles of incarceration. What appears obvious and understandable to them is that their parent is gone, that they have been abandoned and rejected, and are therefore not loved. Among the children of incarcerated parents I have worked with, the most significant feelings I've encountered are those of rejection. When a parent is taken away, the children feel abandoned. The reason as to *why* a parent has left doesn't matter; it is beyond a child's understanding and takes a back seat to the simple fact that the parent is gone and will no longer be involved in the child's day-to-day life.

The emotions that surround an abandoned and rejected child are overwhelming. The child feels guilt for something he or she had no control over—simply because it is a child's nature to be egocentric. These children believe they are to blame. A lack of trust and the loss they feel at being left behind bring on instability and feelings of betrayal. And, of course, shame. When a parent is convicted of a crime, a child is left without a parent. They are alone: alone at their school play, alone at their birthday party, and alone when they go to bed at night.

But regardless of where the parent is in a child's life, the child loves that parent. In situation after situation, I witnessed the incredible strength of that bond. And yet, at the same time, while I certainly expected that a relationship between incarcerated parents and their children would be complicated, what surprised me was the *level* of heartbreak that existed, the tremendous hidden pain of imprisonment. It seems to me that our society should start by attempting to understand the complex bond between children and their incarcerated parents as we work to be conscious of what these children are facing.

It is well known that children suffer most in their lives from failed or failing relationships, from isolation and alienation. "Who is the best person to care for my child?" asked Dr. Lee Salk in his 1972 book *What Every Child Would Like His Parents to Know*. Dr. Salk answered his question by writing, "The best person to care for any child is his parent. Regardless of how well-trained or how well-meaning other people may be, they are not likely to have the deep attachment you have for your own children. The protective feelings that biological parents have for their children are essential for the propagation of the species. Undoubtedly, they have been crucial to the survival of the human race…"

While I still believe that a healthy, biological parent-child relationship is the ideal family dynamic, Dr. Salk's early-1970's enthusiasm has certainly been given a reality check in the 21st century. Today, the issue is not so black and white. After all, there are plenty of stepparents and adoptive parents out there who are doing a much better job raising their children than their biological counterparts. Not to mention grandparents, aunts, uncles, godparents. . . . Regardless, there is certainly no doubt that while many children of imprisoned parents form strong family bonds with other parents and caregivers, absentee parents—imprisoned, unavailable, or unidentified—remain undeniably important to the children they leave behind.

I want to share a letter I received after an article I wrote about my visit to Attica Prison was published. It offers another perspective on the complexities of the issue:

Dear Ms. Martone,

Recently a friend of mine sent me a copy of the article/essay which you wrote for the *Democrat and Chronicle* that was published on Sunday, July 8th. As an "incarcerated co-parent," the article touched me deeply. I don't know if you will ever be able to fully understand just what it was you did, and how much it meant to the incarcerated father and his child. Your generosity, kindness and desire to understand the issues that affect your charges development are extremely rare in today's society. To call you a "hero" would be like calling Babe Ruth "just another baseball player".

Do you have any idea what you did for us as incarcerated parents? You showed society something we inside can't. That being that we love our children, that we care, that we didn't come to jail to "escape the responsibilities of parenting/fatherhood." Personally, I can never thank you enough for that alone, for showing us as "Humans."

On July 4, 1995 I was arrested for burglaries I committed to sustain a cocaine addiction. I had a daughter who was just over 2 yrs old at the time. Was getting arrested my "rock bottom?" No, that came a year later.

My daughter's mother took her for studio pictures. When I received a copy, Sara looked like she was pouting. In the letter that came with the photo was an explanation. "We kept saying smile for daddy, this is for daddy, smile Sara, smile for daddy!" Her response was, "I no smile, daddy not here!!" and with that she proceeded to pout for the camera.

Since that day I have been involved with "parenting issues." Eventually I developed an "Incarcerated Co-Parenting" program at Elmira Correction facility through their Veterans Self Help Development program. I was overwhelmed with the response I got from those who were interested in taking it. That was in '97. Now I am at Livingston Correction Facility (still serving my 8–16 year sentence from '95) and with the help of a very caring counselor here I am setting up my 4th Incarcerated Co-Parenting program. I urge the fathers in my seminar to do as your students father did, write to the schools for information and assistance in regards to growth, health, welfare and development of the child, and what areas he can assist in/increase involvement in. Fortunately, as a result of my commitment to being the best dad I can be for myself first and my daughter second, Sara and I share a depth of love, understanding, acceptance and forgiveness that even fathers who are physically present don't share.

But the letter isn't about me. It is about recognizing you for the beautiful gift you gave to a father and child, the gift of time together. Do you know how a child measures love? Love equals time. I can say with certainty that that little girl (and her father) "love you." My love and respect go out to you as well, from one human recognizing the kindness and selflessness of another. Congratulations Ms. Martone, you've crossed a boundary where few if any dare to tread.

Prayerfully,

When I first read this letter, I could feel the depth of the father's regret for the mistakes he had made. Any potential he may have to be a productive parent is dormant, as far as his child is concerned. For this prisoner, the completion of his sentence offers the possibility of beginning a journey that could save the child from the sins of the father.

The children depicted in these pages are already displaying "personality distortions" which are being manifested insidiously, e.g., poor performance in school, lack of interest in class activities, difficult to handle in class, etc. These cries for help are muted in our current educational system by the lack of teachers with the time and expertise to deal with their problems.

Is there hope for these children? I believe that parent-child contact and the services society can provide to strengthen the unexplainable yet fascinating bond that even bars can't weaken may one day help to break the predictable cycle of imprisonment that is all too often the end result for children whose parents are in prison. Together we *can* foster these bonds between parent and child, ties that can play a crucial role in keeping a parent from returning to prison once they've been released. Even more importantly, fostering this bond can decrease the statistics of these children following in their parents' footsteps.

Thomas Lewis calls humans the "fragile species." The most fragile among us are our children, whom we must protect, guard, and guide for the preservation of our species. That is why, as Jacob Bronowski explains in *The Ascent of Man,* "In our evolutionary ascent, humans are the only species that developed a 'long childhood.' For the Man is the product of the Child." You could not get a human being to build anything unless the child had put together a set of bricks. That is the beginning of the Parthenon and the Taj Mahal, of the Dome at Sultaniyeh and the Watts Towers, of Machu Picchu and the Golden Gate Bridge.

And so it is my hope that the stories of the children in this book will give you a glimpse into their world. I hope I can show you the stigma, shame, and fear that the children feel, and a look into the soul of the prisoners since one cannot be separated from the other. The stories will give a searing and poignant view of what it means to love through bars, and will hopefully present an objective view of the problems as well as a starting place for societal response.

Please enter the world of children with parents in prison through the pages of this book with an open mind. What you do after you get to know them is up to you.

For the purposes of this book, the moral and ethical issues that surround the prison system are less relevant than the care we take to ensure each child's future. What is important is how we can make a difference, "one child at a time."

A Child in a Cell without Bars

I AM WRITING TO YOU concerning my children April in second grade and Joseph in first who attend your school. As you can see by my return address I'm currently incarcerated. I still have all my parental rights and have concerns with my children's education. I would like to know what I need to do to be able to obtain academic and medical records concerning my children periodically. Also the names of their teachers, counselors, and a name of a contact that I can address concerns to as they arise. Please let me know exactly what steps I need to take to obtain this information and maintain an active role in my children's education and well being. I would like to thank you in advance for your time and concern in this matter. I look forward to hearing from you in the near future.

Sincerely,
Steven

As my school counselor shared this letter with me and explained that April and Joseph paid regular visits to their father at Attica prison where he was incarcerated, I was filled with confusion and wonder. My perception of Attica was entirely formed by the infamous 1971 riot. Everything I had ever read or heard about this prison was extremely disturbing. The riot was nothing short of a blood-bath: 1,200 inmates gained control of the prison in a well-planned, savage attack. Fifty correctional officers and civilian employees were brutally beaten and taken hostage. It ended with National Guard helicopters flying overhead, shooting chemical agents, and a rescue force of nearly 200 New York State police officers and two correctional officers storming the facility. The entire rescue operation lasted only several minutes, but was filled with terror and bloodshed. When it was over, 32 inmates and 10 hostages were dead.

Rereading the letter from Steven and contemplating the idea of April and Joseph visiting him there sent a chill up my spine. Compassion overwhelmed me. I had to try and walk in these children's shoes. What would it be like if my father were in prison? I had to know how families dealt with such a situation.

I did some research, and discovered that millions of American children have a parent in prison, and that statistically, these children are much more likely than their classmates to end up incarcerated themselves. I decided then and there that I had to go to that prison with April and Joseph to learn more about this extraordinary—but not, apparently, rare—situation. Perhaps there was a way for me to help not only April and Joseph, but the other children who were faced with the same set of circumstances. At the very least, I could expose this neglected segment of the population to the rest of the world, and initiate a dialogue that would eventually stop the vicious cycle that sees children with parents in prison follow in their father's and/or mother's footsteps. Maybe by writing about such children I could help to initiate a societal response.

I called the children's mother, Diane, introduced myself as the principal of her children's school, and explained that I would like to accompany April and Joseph on one of their visits to see their father. She asked me why and I told her about my own needs for knowing and understanding. I could hear the wonderment in her voice as she queried me on when I would like to do this. "As soon as possible," I replied.

I was surprised to learn that Diane and Steven were not married, but the children were theirs together. I was impressed that she would often take the children to the prison to visit their father, and I commended her for realizing how important it was for Steven to be involved in the children's lives. I hung up the phone feeling certain of the love she felt for her children, as well as for her unselfish ability to put aside her own feelings about Steven for the sake of her children. We made arrangements for the following Sunday, just four days away. Diane would drop the children off on her way to work and would give me the required paperwork to get into the prison. April and Joseph were elated and proceeded to tell their classmates and everyone else of their upcoming day with the school principal.

I wanted to learn more about Steven, so I researched the details of his imprisonment. Steven's rap sheet began with a series of crimes he committed as a teenager: robbery, breaking and entering, car theft, and finally attempted murder while he was actually in prison. His sentence was for a number of years, although no one I spoke with seemed to know exactly how many.

I also learned that his sister's daughter was a student at my school. His sister, Rochelle, was overwhelmed that I would do such a thing for her brother and his children, and she offered all of her assistance in making my journey easier. He certainly was fortunate to have a sister like her. Rochelle had spent some time volunteering in the school but we never really had an opportunity to talk, so I invited her down to my office. She again expressed her joy at my offer to take her brother's children to the prison for a visit.

"I am very concerned about April and Joseph and really appreciate the interest you are taking in them," Rochelle said. She was attractive, with a pleasant voice and a great smile. It was also evident that she was a sweet city girl. I liked her right away.

"I'm grateful that their mother is giving me permission to take the children to visit their father," I replied. "I admire her love for them. I have to tell you that I am amazed by the entire idea, I simply had no sense of how common this situation is and I appreciate your support in helping me to understand. Have you had a chance to talk to your brother since you found out I was taking them to visit him this Sunday?"

"Yeah, and he is nervous about meeting you but glad you are interested in his kids."

"Great! When I get back on Monday, we'll meet and I'll fill you in on how it went."

It was a long four days; I was a little keyed up. Sunday finally rolled around, and I drove over to the local Burger King where I had agreed to meet Diane and the children. However, when I arrived I was surprised to see only April and Diane.

"Hi. It's so nice to meet you," I said to Diane.

"Likewise," Diane replied kindly. She was a tall, plain woman and soft-spoken. April clearly resembled her mother.

"Where is Joseph?" I asked

"He's at home playing with his cousins and didn't feel like coming today," Diane replied.

"Well, maybe next time," I said, trying to mask my disappointment.

Diane seemed relieved that she didn't have to accompany April on this visit. April, on the other hand, was beaming, and made no effort to hide how happy she was to be going to Attica. She was all dressed up in a pink sundress, her blonde hair pulled back in a ponytail. She had even painted her fingernails for the occasion! "Wow, you look beautiful," I said, giving her a hug.

"Thank you," she replied with a big smile on her face.

Diane handed me the required paperwork: Steven's prison number, a permission slip, and April's birth certificate, all folded up in a plastic sandwich bag. She told me that she had written to Steven and he was expecting us. She thanked me, kissed and hugged April, and was on her way.

"April, I'm a little hungry. Why don't we have breakfast before we go?"

"Pancakes for me!" she blurted out.

The drive up to Attica was somewhat quiet, and at one point I thought April was going to fall asleep. She was tired, I suspected, from having to meet me at seven in the morning. It took us a little over two hours, which included a stop at a gas station for directions; Attica was not an easy place to find.

Finally, as I came around the bend in the road, the prison towered in front of us. We pulled into the parking lot and parked the car. When we got out and started walking, a guard with a gun in his hand yelled, "You can't park there! Park down there." And he motioned to another area with his gun.

We got back in the car and went over to where some other visitors were parking. As we walked toward the gate, I began taking pictures of the complex with my camera.

"Lady! No cameras allowed," the guard yelled. I was not exactly prison-savvy.

We walked back to the car, dropped off the camera, and were then picked up by a van that took us to a processing center. The entire time, April hardly said two words.

Inside, there was a desk with sign-up sheets requesting the prisoner to be visited, his number, and who we were. I was overwhelmed by this experience; it was so out of the realm of things I'd ever done. I'm sure my expression of total bewilderment prompted the woman in attendance to ask who I was. Before I could respond, April shouted out, "She's my principal!" This was a proclamation I was glad she so loudly made; it helped to relieve the tension that had been building up. We received a number, took a seat, and waited for our turn.

The room was filled with tables and chairs. In one corner there was a small kitchen area with drinks and snacks, while another corner had a TV set. Long benches set in every direction filled the room.

"I'm hungry," April chimed, as she hopped up and walked to the kitchen where she helped herself to dry cereal in a cup. I debated as to whether to allow her to do this since the place wasn't very clean. "Ms. M, do you want some cereal?" She handed me the white Dixie cup filled with Fruit Loops.

"No thanks," I smiled. I kept thinking about what she was being exposed to; I certainly would never want this for my grandson.

More and more people began entering the room, and I have to admit it was a bit like watching a freak show: there were more tattoos, over-painted faces of thick crusted make-up, excessive cleavage, and pierced earrings on every body part imaginable in this one room than I had seen in my entire life. And the level of crude conversations and swearing was staggering. These were things eight-year-old girls should not have to experience. I had an overwhelming urge to grab her and run. Yet, watching April, she seemed oblivious to all this, as though it were completely normal.

Finally, forty-five minutes later, they called our number and we were escorted to a van where we were crammed in for the short drive to the main gate. The odors of cheap perfume and cologne in the hot, ten-passenger van made me feel sick.

"I hope the ride is a short one," I whispered in her ear.

"It is," April whispered back.

Herded like cattle, we were led through the main gate of the prison where we entered another holding room. To the left of us was a long counter with guards standing behind it. They told us to take a seat. At the end of the counter stood a metal detector. The room had two long rows of benches off to the right where we sat and waited. In front of us, one guard sat behind a piece of glass in front of a control panel. One by one the prisoners' names were called.

A young, very handsome Latin man dressed in a Marine uniform began to take his military jacket off to hand to the guard when a woman yelled out, "Take it all off, honey!"

As each name was called, we watched the visitor remove his possessions and shoes, and walk through the metal detector. Once they passed through, the guard would return their belongings. We sat and waited until Steven's name was finally called and we too removed all of our jewelry and our shoes. Once cleared, the guard returned our items and a barred gray metal door eerily clanged open. As we stepped into a chamber the door slammed shut behind us. I grabbed April's hand. A guard sitting behind a glass window watched every move we made. I nodded to him. He made no response, not even a gesture.

The next barred metal door opened and April and I walked out. A path led us through to the building that housed the visiting area. There were bars on the windows in a building off to my left. "There's the trailer we stay at when we visit my dad on the weekend," April said quietly. A chain-link fence surrounded several white double-wide trailers. I wanted to take a closer look, but thought I had better not deviate from our path and risk the wrath of the guards.

We walked through a series of corridors, like a maze, with white-painted walls and gray-painted floors. The windows were high and only allowed light in; we couldn't see outside. Entering the room in the visiting area was a surprise and not at all what I expected. The walls were beautifully painted with Disney characters. Directly to the left, there were a multitude of vending machines and microwaves, as it was not permissible to bring in food or other items. Another corner housed a play area for children, with tables and toys.

In another area, an inmate was taking Polaroid pictures of other inmates with their guests. The room was filled with about fifty square tables where inmates were sitting with their families and friends. You knew the prisoners not only by their green-colored pants, but also by their assigned seats, which, without exception, faced the guards. We approached two guards sitting behind a tall booth.

One of the guards assigned us to a table where we sat and waited. One by one an inmate would be allowed to enter the room to join his visitors. I was so anxious I could have burst out of my skin each time the steel gray door opened. "Is that him?" I would ask April. She was so calm and, as always, just smiled at me. She had been like this for the entire trip. Usually, little girls her age are non-stop talkers, but she was quiet. Quiet to the point that it felt a bit unsettling.

Waiting for Steven to emerge from behind the closed metal doors, I couldn't help but get caught up in what I was seeing. There was a great deal of noise as prisoners entered the room. They were all well dressed and neat, hugging their visitors. One couple was necking so passionately, their heads going round and round, that they made me dizzy. There was no shame in this room; anything and everything went. The children were running around and playing in the corner with toys, and a mix of laughter and crying filled the room. Finally, the door opened again and Steven came out.

"There he is," April screamed, her face radiating her unconditional love for him. I on the other hand was shocked to say the least; he was not at all what I expected. Steven was handsome and well built, with blonde hair and blue eyes. He was wearing a blue shirt that reflected every feature of his muscular body. This certainly wasn't the typical prisoner I was expecting to see.

He barely had time to sit before April jumped onto his lap. We introduced ourselves; I could sense he was nervous about the visit. I tried to put him at ease. "Please call me Cynthia," I said.

"Ever since they told me you were coming, I've been very nervous about meeting you," Steven began. "I appreciate what you're doing for my children. It was nice of you to bring my daughter to see me." He had such a pleasant, articulate voice. April noticed every detail about his face, touching his nose, rubbing his cheeks, playing with the hair on his wrists and stroking his shoulder.

"Dad, did you notice my new hairstyle?" she asked.

"How is your brother, and mom, and how are you doing at school?" he gently coaxed her.

She nodded, "they're OK," and then her direction shifted to me. "Ms. M., did you know that Mark Chapman was here?" Steven pointed to the cell; I looked in that direction. "He killed John Lennon. My mom loves his music."

"Steven, I just read the book *Let Me Take You Down* by Jack Jones. It's an interesting work and would give you some insight into Mark Chapman, his life, and the reasons why he killed John Lennon. It is an enthralling story."

"He is considered rather special here at the prison and is in an area where others can't get to him," Steven told me. "I saw him once when I was walking in the hall."

Steven and I were both surprised to see Steven's sister and her daughter walking around the corner. She never gave any indication to either of us that she was coming.

"I didn't know you were coming. Why don't you sit here with us?" I commented.

"I can't," Rochelle replied. "Each prisoner is allowed only three visitors. I just decided to come up at the last minute and thought I would visit Tom since he seldom gets any company. He has no family here." The door opened and Tom walked in, came to the table and sat with them. It was like a family reunion. Steven proceeded to tell me that Tom had accidentally killed a man in a brawl. Tom, too, was a nice-looking young man, tall, well built with very long hair pulled into a ponytail, and from the look on his face he was obviously very happy to have visitors. Steven introduced him to me and told him who I was. Tom smiled and nodded to me.

"Very nice to meet you," I said.

I was surprised to learn from Steven that the prison system allows families to visit the inmates for a long weekend, generally about every six to eight weeks. They are responsible for bringing their own food and any other supplies necessary, almost like camping. Once in the prison they are only permitted to leave if they become sick and require medical attention. The weekend turns into family picnics with prisoners sharing the space behind the fence, while gun-carrying guards watch every move from the towers above.

"Steven, these walls are beautiful and so colorful. Who painted the Disney figures?"

Steven pointed to one of the artists three tables away.

"Why is he here?" I asked.

"He killed his wife, her boyfriend and her attorney, in the attorney's office."

I just shook my head. I couldn't help staring and wondering how a man could kill another human being, let alone three at one time.

"Dad, we're hungry, " said April as her aunt gave them some money for the vending machines. The girls just amazed me; it was as though they had always been in this environment. No fear, apprehension or concern with the caliber of people they were with. I just could not understand the openness of being in this environment as though it were normal.

"Cynthia," Steven began, "I made a lot of mistakes, and did a lot of dumb things. I stole things, broke into houses, ran from parole. I never killed anyone and I never understood why I ended up here at Attica. Do you know it costs $36,000 to house a prisoner for a year? One thing's for sure, I've learned a lot. I'm trying to do a lot of positive things while I'm here. I've been an asset to the Corcraft metal shop, working as a drafts-man drawing all the blueprints for the last three years. I'm also a volunteer in the ALFA program, a youth assistance program conducted by inmates who work with schools, probation and police departments, and youth agencies. Every Monday, outside agencies bring in about 20 kids, ranging from 12-21 years old. Paul oversees this program. Maybe if you call him, you can come for an evening and talk to the students."

I listened intently to every word he spoke, watching every move he made. There was no self-pity in his voice, just a desire to do what he had to until his release, and then be the father he hadn't been able to be. I couldn't help thinking that, regardless of the situation, parents play such a crucial role in the lives of their children.

We talked of things I would be able to do as an administrator to help bridge Steven and his children's lives—at least as far as their education was concerned. "Steven, when I go back to school on Monday, I will meet with the teachers and set up a parent/teacher conference via the phone. I will also send you the children's schoolwork and information regarding classroom activities. I can see how much your children love you, and you them, and I will support them in missing a few days of schools every six to eight weeks in order to spend an extended weekend with you. I also need your help. When they are here it's important that you stress academics. April and Joseph need to do their homework and you need to read to them and they to you. It just can't be all fun and games. Your children are struggling academically and need all the help they can get. If you want, you can send cards and notes and I will see that they get them. Regardless of the fact that you're in prison, there's no time to be a fairy tale dad because you feel guilty for not being there."

In his quiet voice he replied, "I will, I promise. No one has ever done this for me, I won't let you down or them. Cynthia, would you mind having a picture taken with all of us?" he asked. I went with them to the corner of the room where an inmate was taking Polaroid pictures for five dollars. I was a little taken back when Steven put his arm around me and gently pulled me toward him with April in front of us both.

Back at the table, I thanked him for such a nice visit. I felt a little awkward since I could feel that he didn't want the visit to end. He handed me a slip of paper.

"Cynthia, I made something for you. On your way out, give this paper to the guard." I thanked him again and watched as he and April embraced. On my way out I stopped at the door where the guard stood behind a counter, I handed him the paper Steven had given me. The guard, in turn, handed me an envelope. To my surprise, Steven had hand-crafted a token of his appreciation, a beautiful card! "Thank you, from the bottom of my heart." Opening the card a little yellow bear popped up. I walked out feeling so confused, feeling good, wanting to cry, glad to be leaving, yet wanting to stay longer. Certainly, much differently than when I walked in.

At school on Monday morning everyone wanted to know what had happened. But the only thing I wanted to do was get the ball rolling. I called April and Joseph's teachers down to my office. "I want to meet with both of you when we have time to really talk so that I can let you know what happened yesterday. I want to make sure that we include him as though he were just living down the street. Yesterday was very touching for me and it opened my eyes. We should make every effort to do parent-teacher conferences over the phone and let's send him as much of the children's homework, tests, and projects as possible."

The teachers quickly said they would be happy to do anything to help, and didn't have a problem including him in the loop.

That afternoon we sent the first package of the children's work and photos to Steven. Unbeknownst to me, April's teacher also included a letter that explained the academic difficulties the child was having in school this year and her contemplation of whether April should be retained since she was so far behind.

Three days later a letter arrived postmarked Attica Correctional Facility.

Dear Ms. Martone:

I cannot thank you enough. It was a act of courage on your part to make the trip here. You are a very determined, energetic person. I admire your style. It was a blessing for me, to have you take the time out of your day to bring April up to see me. April loves you; you really made a very enthusiastic impression. April was very excited about you bringing her up. I was disappointed my son did not come. I'm not very good at expressing myself in writing. I really felt like crying a few times. I was able to hold it til I was in private. The whole event left me bristling with so many things to think about. "There is no synthetic replacement for a decent home life." I've been a big embarrassment to my children and family. I have failed in a lot of ways, and I realize I can't change the past but I'm working hard for the future. I love my children and only want the best for them. I grasp every memory I have of my children in my mind, heart and soul to over come every dark day I face. I'm very grateful for your sensitivity to our involuntary separation.

I'd be interested in getting a copy of the article you write. I'll be taking a test may 24, to enroll in the Consortium College Program, to enroll in the summer semester. I'm excited about that. Well thanks again, and I'll keep in touch.

Respectfully,
Steven

I was so touched, I just sat there. At least we were on our way for these two children. This entire experience was so overwhelmingly emotional. Two days later, another letter arrived. This time it was sent to April's teacher.

"Cynthia, I just received a letter from April's father and I think you better read it." She handed me the letter and walked back to her classroom.

Dear Teacher,

First I'd like to thank you for taking the time to write me, and provide me with some of my daughter's schoolwork. I save every little thing I get from both of my children. I love my children and I have made every effort to stay active and involved in their lives, academic advancement. I have followed my daughter's progress from Kindergarten to the present.

Further, I was deeply alarmed about your letter, I respect your concern about April in the areas you outlined namely, math, reading skills. I realize you may believe holding April back a year will help her better advance in those areas. April has been faced with so many things. Such as me not being there, and adjusting to another man in her mothers life has caused a great deal of confusion in her little world. April has not failed, it is her father who has failed.

I can not agree with you about holding April back a year.

I OPPOSE this for a number of reasons:

1) This will delay April's education a year,

2) This will place April in the same grade as her younger brother Joseph, Setting her back a year would only cause more emotional problems. Namely what she would go through. As kids she has grown up with go ahead, and shes left behind, which would lead to her being picked on by her class mates, and possibly by her little brothers class mates. I am willing to make arrangements to get April extra help in the areas needed, and I believe April can over come this obstacle. I have faith in April. I have addressed my concern with April's mother and I believe she will be in agreement with me. Their is a wonderful loving mother and I have a lot of respect for her. We both want what is best for both our children.

I feel it would be best to move April on to the third grade and work with her in areas you have outlined in your letter. I'll discuss this with my daughter and her mother. I do respect your thinking, please don't misunderstand me I only want what is best for April and I speak from experience. I was held back in the second grade and I went through everything mentioned above. I'm open to any suggestions you may have. I have made arrangements for April and my son Joseph to go to Florida this summer, they will be spending time with my mother and my older brother Jim and his wife. I will speak to them about this and the areas April needs to work on. I realize I'm limeted in April" every day life, but there is not a day that goes by without me thinking about my children, and I know I'm missing a great deal, and I regret that. I can only be a long distance dad, but I'm not a dead beat father. I will do everything I can to help make a difference. I'd like to thank you for your time and attention to this situation.

Respectfully,
Steven

I immediately went down to the classroom. "There will be no retention taking place while I'm here," I said to April's teacher. "It is the worst thing that can happen to a child. There is significant research that has shown it does not work. If she is having problems then let's get her the help she needs. Let's set up a conference with her mom and see if summer school can be an option."

Later that afternoon my secretary announced that there was a phone call from Attica Prison. I was surprised to hear from a woman who introduced herself as Sister Agatha.

"Ms. Martone, my name is Sister Agatha and I called to tell you how wonderful you are. I run the ministries here at the prison and no one has ever done anything like this. You are an incredible person and an angel. You are in our prayers. I am going to put Steven on the phone to talk with you. God bless you!"

Steven's voice was gracious. "Ms. Martone, I want to thank you again for all you are doing for me and my children. Like Sister Agatha said, you are an angel. She was really impressed with what you did and wanted to talk with you herself. Did you get my letter?"

"Yes," I said, "and April will not be retained if you can assure me that your family will support her over the summer. We will get some practice books together along with some ideas that will help increase her skills. Please stress to them the importance of this and tell them they can call me. I will be happy to help in any way that I can."

Abruptly, he said, "My time is up, I have to hang up. I will write again. Thank you."

"Wait," I yelled. "When can we talk again?"

"I am not sure but I will talk with Sister Agatha and try to call again," he replied in that soft-spoken voice of his.

Two days later another letter arrived:

Dear Cynthia,

It was a blessing to speak to you and April's teacher on the phone. I'm deeply touched by your commitment to the children you over see. I had no ideal April was having problems in school till I read the letter her teacher had inclosed with all the pitchers, and April's school work. I'll be honest I had to get off the phone because I was so over come with emotion, you have really encouraged me to take a more active roll with in April, and Joseph's education. I only wish I would of known April was having a problem earlier in the year. I have been in contact with my mother. I spoke to her and my brother and his wife regarding the areas of concern with April. I had asked my mother to call you or the teacher to confirm, and reinforce what I had said on the phone, about helping April advance in the areas of concern. April and Joseph will be spending the summer with my mother and my older brother's family. I assure you April will get some extra help this summer, and if she needs extra help next year I will make arrangements for her to get it.

I can't thank you enough. I love my children. I want them to always know that. Sister Agatha was so touched by everything I had told her about your visit, the pitchers, ECT. I did not expect to call the school that day, but I sure was happy it worked out that way.

Actions speak louder than words, and your actions say a lot. I can tell you're a very loving, caring person. I appreciate your compliment on my writing. I speak from the heart, open and honestly, and when talk to anyone I always look them in the eye, because the eyes are the windows to a persons soul. My father always told us that. I realize me and the kids have a lot of challenges ahead of us. I can't say I have all that it will take, I will do everything I can for my children. The whole nightmare has been a emotional, mental demolition derby. I realize time stands still for no-one and we just have to make the best of what we have right now. The kids and my sister will be up for a week-end visit June 14th thru the 16th. The 14th is my birthday so to me it's a wonderful birthday present. "Thank you so much". Every thing you have done means so much to me!

Respectfully,
Steven

Over the next few months, many changes took place, including my accepting a new position at a school hundreds of miles away in Pennsylvania. I was extremely excited about moving forward, yet apprehensive about whether or not the things I had initiated would be followed through. With my new job and responsibilities to a whole different group of children, I knew I wouldn't be able to stay involved in Steven, April, and Joseph's lives, and I worried that the subsequent administration would drop the ball. I hoped the children's new teachers and principal would understand the special circumstances surrounding not only April and Joseph but all the children who had a parent in prison, and made it a special point to share my concerns with everyone involved. Word had gotten back to Steven about my impending move, and another letter arrived shortly after my announcement.

Bonjour Ms. Martone,

I realize this maybe the last time I'm able to communicate with you. I'm sad to see you go. It's not every day you meet someone special, and as willing to take step in faith to help fill a gap in someone's life. Everything you have

said, and done has been one of the most
encouraging.

I realize you must have said something to
their mother because the kids brought in me
in school pitchers of them from this year. I've
been blessed with two beautiful loving children,
and it's been a very devastating experience for
all of us, and I just look forward to day I can be
a full time daddy again. Till then I'll make the
most of what I have. If it's not to much to ask,
when you get the pitchers back from our visit
could you please send me a copy.

If I can ever be of any assistance to you in
anyway, don't hesitate to ask. I wish you the
best, and take care.

Respectfully,
Steven

A year passed, and I must admit that I became guilty
of letting the hustle and bustle of life engulf me. I had
wondered over the year about how things were going
with Steven and the children and would make myself
notes to call those involved in the situation. Finally, after
calling the school, I was able to touch base with Steven's
sister, Rochelle. It was a phone call I wish I hadn't placed.
It saddened me to learn that all of the progress we had
made had gone in vain and to learn that Steven was
moved to another correctional facility, a facility less
restrictive for the prisoners but more restrictive when it
came to visits from family members. The children were
still struggling academically but seemed to be manag-

ing; there were no significant problems. But there were also no parent-teacher conferences over the phone, and the mailing of schoolwork and teacher correspondence with Steven had come to a complete halt. It crushed me even more to learn that the children had not seen him in three months.

"Everything in vain," I sat and cried.

My Little Queen, My Little Princess

NATALIE IS A STUNNING YOUNG woman of Puerto Rican and Italian decent. Her rich, dark skin, and her black hair pulled into a bun on top of her head add to her beauty. At 17 years old, she is a well-developed young woman. Upon noticing that her left eyebrow was pierced, I asked her if her eyebrow hurt. She shook her head, and then simultaneously stuck out her tongue and lifted her shirt to reveal a pierced tongue as well as a fish-like charm dangling from her belly button. While observing the multiple piercings, I also noticed a scar on Natalie's face. She shared with me the story of the fight she had gotten into at school with another girl which resulted in her getting suspended. It was the result of one of those "she said, he said" arguments.

It was apparent that Natalie lived a hard life filled with drugs and all that goes along with that atmosphere. As we sat together with her mother, Maria, I learned of the mistakes her mom had made and the impact they had had upon Natalie. Throughout the course of our conversation, their story detailed a life filled with drugs.

"If you think it's hard seeing one parent taken away to prison," Maria asked, "imagine a child having to see two 'role models' in her life handcuffed at gun point and taken away."

"My real dad and my stepdad," Natalie clarified. "I saw them both arrested and taken to jail."

Her mother felt compelled to interject and share with me the mistakes she has made. "When she was three, I met a man—her stepfather—Ricardo. He was from Puerto Rico. He had no money, so he decided he was gonna sell drugs. He knew it was a way to make good money. My daughter fortunately didn't know anything that was going on back then. But as she got older, Ricardo kept getting bigger and bigger—selling more drugs and making more money. Finally, one day Natalie experienced the police kicking our door in, kicking her stepfather, and saw me on the floor with a gun to my head."

Natalie began to fill in the details: "I was only six years old at the time but I will never forget that night; it was like it happened yesterday. I was in bed and I heard a bunch of noise that scared me. I went to see what was happening and as I was walking down the hallway a cop was walking towards me with a gun pointed at me. He started screaming, 'Who is it? Who's coming? I hear somebody.' Other officers came into the hallway and I started screaming. The police officer picked me up and carried me out into the living room. I saw my mom and stepdad on the floor; the police had handcuffed them and had guns to their heads. I was crying so hard they let my mom sit on the couch with me. The walls were all broken; I learned they were looking for money and drugs inside the walls. The police took my stepfather and they left me and my mom alone, they only wanted him. We had to put a sheet up to cover the door because we had no door. We didn't sleep the whole night because we didn't know if the police would be back. All of this because of the drugs." She sat there shaking her head.

"There were so many incidents I saw. There was another time my mom, stepdad and me were driving around and an undercover cop was following us. My mom tried to tell Ricardo, 'You know, someone's following us. I've seen this car more than one time.' He wouldn't listen to her and would say, 'No, no, we're fine, we're fine.' Well, we were driving down a street and all of a sudden a bunch of cops came right to the car and stopped us. My stepdad got out of the car and started running, and I saw him jump over a fence. I was sitting in the backseat and the police had my mom behind the car, handcuffed, with a gun to her head. The cops were yelling, 'What's his name? Why'd he run? Who is it?' The cops tried to get information out of her and I just sat in the car."

Her mother spoke up, "Actually, they threatened to take my daughter from me so I told them what they wanted to hear. They took me downtown; a female officer stayed with my daughter. All they wanted to know was more about Ricardo. I later learned that Ricardo was making a deal with a guy who was wired and working for the police.

"After that day and the threat of the police taking my daughter from me, I allowed no more—the money or the drugs—in my house. I stopped it from there on out. Ricardo still gave me money and supported us, but whatever he did, it was away from my house. He kept selling the drugs after that but not as big as he was before, and Ricardo did his drug stuff in somebody else's house. He ended up getting caught again and taken to jail. This time they gave him an option of probation. He was under house arrest for a couple of years and had to wear a bracelet on his ankle so that he couldn't leave his house. If he left his house, his bracelet beeped and notified the police. Actually, he did good on that; he didn't mess that up at all."

"My stepdad," Natalie interjected, "he went to college to be an accountant. He was very intelligent and he graduated from college." She was so proud of him in spite of all his shortcomings.

I was curious as to his treatment of his stepdaughter, "What was he like as a stepfather?"

"We lived with my stepdad as a family until I was about 13. I remember when I was younger, he was mean and he didn't really like me. But as I got older, he was strict, but it was for the better. I mean, strict like with school, with boys, with my grades. I would get punished if I didn't have good grades. I wasn't allowed to have a boyfriend until I turned 17. He was good, he was like a... like my father. When people asked me who that is, I said, "my father." I didn't say 'stepfather.' I said it was my father because he raised me. He done everything for me, but he was pretty strict. But now I understand why. When I was younger, I didn't like that and I couldn't understand why he was being so strict. I got mad and I used to tell my mom, 'Why is he so mean to me?' But now, I realize why."

"He was married when I met him," Maria admits. "Which I didn't know. But he did end up leaving his wife. They got a divorce and so on, and so forth. We didn't marry, we just stayed together. I didn't get married and

I didn't have another child. No! He has three of his own biological kids and he was the same way with them. Actually, he was worse with them."

At 17 years old, Natalie could talk about the history of arrests as though it was in a social studies lesson. "And now, he's in prison. I can't even tell you how many years he's doing now. He was taken away and then he got let out. He got caught again, got taken away again, and then got let out. Got caught again, got put on house arrest, got put on probation and they gave him a chance. My stepdad has been in minimum and maximum security prisons. He was working for the police helping them to catch drug dealers. The more he did of that, the less time he had to spend in prison. I remember when he got his notice in the mail telling him when he had to go to a maximum prison in Kentucky. The court sent him to Kentucky because he was ratting on people, so they sent him out of the area because now, the people he ratted on are in prison around here. So, for his protection, they sent him away."

"Have you gone down to visit him?" I asked them both.

"No." They both answered in unison.

"Neither one of us want to. We've been through a lot of ups and downs with him and I think we're ready to let go," Maria replied as they both nodded.

"I've seen my mom suffer a lot for him."

"Does he write to either of you?"

"Not anymore," Natalie answered. "He did, but not anymore. I don't want him to. He's wrote me about four letters. He sent me a birthday card when I turned 17 and after that I haven't received a letter or anything, but I don't want to. He did call me when he got to the prison in Kentucky. He was walking in and he called me from the pay phone just outside the prison wall. He was crying and told me, 'I love you.'"

The young girl spoke in a very soft voice, almost a whisper, "When we lived together, we were all happy. It was wonderful. We would go on vacation, we would go out to eat. When we moved into our own house, we got farther and farther apart from when we lived together. It's just like as the days went on, he went his own way and we went our own way. And now we don't speak at all, really."

"Does he call you from the prison?"

"He got his phone privileges taken away for two years and he was put into a 'box.' He's in a box now, for 30 days just stuck up in a little box. If you do something wrong in a prison they put you into a box. When you are in prison, you're allowed a phone card with 400 minutes on it a month. If you go over those minutes, you cannot get any more. Well, he decided he was going to get a card in his friend's name. You are not allowed to do that and they caught him. In the box, means: 24 hours in, and one hour out—every day. So, 23 hours in the box, one hour out a day. It's four walls, a bed, and toilet.

"We were with him the day that he left. Me, my mother and his children were at his house saying good-bye to him before he went. We were all crying and he was saying his good-byes and telling me he's proud of me, keep going to school and take care of your mom, be there for each other. It was hard for me then. I cried and I was sad. But now, no, I don't feel bad that he's in there by himself."

Maria picked up: "I had gotten pregnant as soon as I met her biological father. I had her and then 2 1/2 years later I met Ricardo. I met Ricardo, her stepfather, after her biological father, Jose, went to jail for burglary. Her real dad used to use a lot of drugs and I didn't know it when I met him. After he went to jail, I lost all contact with him but I still saw his mother. For 13 years we would see him in the street and he would come to the car to say, 'Hi,' give his daughter a kiss and take off.

"For a long time Ricardo wanted to adopt her—"

"And I'm glad you didn't let him do that," Natalie interrupted. "My father had to sign a paper. He didn't want to sign it."

"The paper never got to him because I kinda stopped it," Maria said. "For 13 years we'd see him in the street hanging out, whatever. He'd go back to jail, come out, back and forth."

"What jail was he in?" I asked.

"Oh, he's been in Attica, Groveland. I mean he's been in all of them. When Natalie was little I used to bring her."

"The last time I saw my dad I was 13," Natalie remembered. "My mom and I were driving down Clinton Avenue and he was walking up Clinton Avenue. My mom rolled the window down and she goes, 'Nat, there's your father.' I turned my head to look at him, as she honked. He looked at the car and he kept walking. My mom honked again and yelled out to him, 'Aren't you going to come look at your daughter?' My dad came to the car, 'Oh, my God, that's my daughter?' She got so big! And he came up and gave me a hug and a kiss and that was it. That was four years ago. He's had no contact with me between then and now.

"One morning, me and my mother were sitting downstairs on the couch watching TV. We always turn the news on, check the weather, see what's going on. We're sitting there watching it and we see this guy getting pulled out of the gorge. He was holding onto a branch. It was freezing and he was frozen. They showed the whole rescue and him getting in the ambulance. He was trying to get into the ambulance and almost fell because he was so cold he couldn't even lift his leg up."

"My mother looked at me and said, 'Nat, that's your father! That's your father!' I knew he was my father, but I didn't know. If I were to seen him, I don't think I would of known who he was until she said to me, 'That's your dad.' But I wouldn't have known who he was if I was watching the TV and my mom wasn't there sitting next to me saying, 'That's your dad.'

"After my mom told me and I saw him on the news being pulled out of the gorge, I told her I want to go see him. And my mom goes, 'Okay.' So that night I went to go pick up my friend to sleep over and I decided to stop at my dad's mother's place, where she worked. I asked one of the women if Rose was here, 'I'm her granddaughter.' She said, 'No, Rose's not here.' I said, 'Well, I'm trying to get in touch with my father, Jose.' The women told me, 'He is at your grandmother's house right now.' So, I said, 'Well, where does my grandmother live?' She told me where they lived. I went over there and I walked in and he was sitting on the couch."

"Wasn't this after quite a few years of not having seen him?" I asked.

"Yeah, the last time I seen him was when I was about 13 and I'm 17 now."

"So I walked in and I go, 'Hi,' and he goes, 'Oh, my God, how are you?' I sat and I talked to him for a little while and we switched phone numbers. We called each other and he ended up getting put back in jail after a couple of weeks. He's in there now. Actually, I talked to him today and he said he was going to court today to find out what's going to happen, if he has to stay in there. We call each other all the time and I went and seen him sometimes. Now he's back in jail."

"My daughter and her father are actually starting a relationship," Maria added, a mixture of surprise, happiness, and concern in her voice.

"A father-daughter relationship—we're trying." The young girl's desperation was tangible.

"How do you know what is going on with your dad right now?"

"He called me the morning he got arrested. It was a collect call from the Monroe County Jail. I knew it was him—he said his name and I accepted the phone call. He told me, 'I'm in jail and I don't know how long I'm going to be in here but I'm here now.' I woke my mom up and I said, 'Mom, my dad's in jail.' And they talked for a couple of minutes and then that was it. He's written us twice, but we haven't been down to see him yet. We will though, because I'm trying to keep in contact with him. I know it's going to be hard for him to call me because he's in jail and I can't call him, so, the way I have to keep in contact is to go visit him. I want to get to know him and want for him to be my father. I can't do that while he's in jail without going to see him. I mean, it's going to be hard for him to be my father while he's in jail, but I want him to know that I care and I do want him to be there for me.

"My father feels real bad that he's in jail again and he can't be there for me. He tells me all the time, 'You know, I haven't been there for you. I want to be your father now. I love you. I miss you. I can't wait to get out. I'm going to change.'

"Well, I think he really does miss me. My dad's mother tells him, 'She knows that you're doing wrong and she wants you to be there for her, and she's not a little girl any more.' His mother always told him, "Your daughter's going to come looking for you one day.' He'd tell me, 'You know, my mom said you were going to come looking for me one day.' I'm glad I did, but I wish he wasn't in jail."

"Do your friends know the situation with your dad?" I asked.

"Two of my friends know and they won't tell anyone. Everything I tell them and everything they tell me we all keep between each other. Just us three. Us three know more about each other than anybody else in our school. When something goes wrong, we all call each other. We're real close. Just us three."

"Are you angry at the way things have turned out?"

"Well, when my stepfather, Ricardo, went away, I was hurt. I was angry because he knows he was doing wrong and he knows he has kids and me. But I was more upset than angry. When he left, like the hug I gave him was not a hug I've never, ever hugged before. It was a 'I'm going to miss you, I love you hug.'

"And when my real father went away, I didn't get to see him because the cops were looking for him and he went to New York City trying to hide. He came back from New York because the person he was staying with didn't want my dad to stay with him anymore. So he came back from New York and went back to his mother's house and a couple of weeks later he ended up getting caught. So I really didn't get to say goodbye to him. But I was upset. I wasn't really angry that he was gone. I was just more upset when I found out that he was in jail.

"I suffered more with my stepdad than I did with my real father, only because Ricardo's been there for me, I know Ricardo, I don't really know my father. All I know is that he is my biological father. He had me and that's pretty much it. I don't really know anything about him."

"Do you feel torn at all that you don't have any contact with your stepfather?"

"I don't want anything to do with him. I don't feel torn. I'm not confused whether I should or shouldn't talk to him. I don't want to and I'm not gonna. I don't want to see him and I don't want to write him. I don't want him to write me. I just want it left at this, and me and my mom will be happy and move on."

"Is it important for you to build a relationship between yourself and your real dad?"

"That's what I want to do. I'd like he and my mom to get back together but only if my dad stops drinking. If he doesn't stop drinking, then I'll just be his daughter and he can be my dad and they can be friends and we'll leave it that. We don't have everything anymore, but I'd rather have what we have now than have it be drug money. And seeing my mom get guns put to her head and handcuffed, and me running around crying. I'd rather it just be like this, just the two of us."

"You've been through a great deal for being just seventeen years old. Is it difficult to put all of this into perspective?"

"I didn't know what to think or do. I was just confused, upset, and saying, 'Why does it have to happen to me? What did I do wrong that this has to happen to me? Why do I have to go through this and see my mother suffer? See my dad get locked up and coming in and out of my life, going to jail and coming back out and saying everything's going to be okay?' It was just confusing, so I didn't know what to think or do. I used to cry a lot and I wrote a lot. I cried and wrote at the same time. I put my music on and I just wrote how I felt."

"If you could have one wish what would that be?"

"I would like to see my mom and dad get back together but only if he stops drinking. If he doesn't stop drinking, no, because he's a violent person when he drinks and I wouldn't want for her to go through what she went through when I was a baby. Now, me being older, I'll be able to watch that and see what happens. If he can come out and he's ready to be a father and he's ready to stop drinking and be a family, yeah, I'd like to see that. But if he can't stop drinking and he's not ready to settle down, then we'll have a father-daughter relationship and they can be friends and that's it."

"When you're at school and people are talking about their fathers what do you say or do?

"I sit there and listen and think, wishing my father could have been that way. Wishing I could have been with my real father and him having a good job. I wish my stepfather didn't put my mother through what he put her through. And just wishing that it could have been me, my mom and my dad, and him having a good job and us be a family. I really don't say much. I just sit and think."

"Do you have any other friends that are in the same situation?"

"No, but I have a boyfriend. He doesn't do drugs. No drinking. No smoking cigarettes. He's perfect. I know he's never cheated on me. He don't even look at other girls. He's done with school. He likes to lay down pavement, like masonry. And he can landscape."

"Don't hide anything from me," Maria suddenly warned her daughter. "Don't sneak. I catch her at a lot of the things when she sneaks. I don't want to catch you. Tell me, you know. I can look at her and usually know something is going on. I've lived it. She's got to remember, I have lived it. I've lived it, you know."

"Are you involved in any sports or activities at school?"

"No. I played softball one time in eighth grade. There's a picture right there on the side of the fridge. I'm lazy. I am. I go to school and I come home and lay down."

"Do you get good grades?"

"I don't right now. I struggle in school. I always have. I always run about a 'C' average. I was sick and I was out of school for a couple of weeks. And then, well, Ricardo went to jail, then I got real sick and started missing school and a lot of things were on my mind. I wasn't focusing on school. I had too much on my mind to focus on school. I'm getting my grades up now. I'm catching up on all my work and I'm doing better now."

"About your real dad—do you know the whole story about the things your dad has been involved with over the years?"

"Yeah, burglarizing, stealing. I can tell you all that. Didn't work. Stole an ambulance. Took off in it."

"Does your real dad have regrets that he wasn't there for you?"

"He said it to me all the time, 'I wish I would have been there. I wish I could be your father, show you that I care and show you that I do want to be your father. There's just a lot going on now.' He regrets it. He told me he wanted to be my father when he gets out. He's ready to be a father. He told me that before, but now I think he knows that I'm older and I'm realizing it's his decision to be my father because I want him to be. You know, before it was up to me, but now I'm showing, 'I do want you to be my father. I do want you to come into my life.' So, it's his decision now."

"And he seems to be taking the steps?"

"Yeah. It's nice to be wanted."

"That's nice that you're going to build that relationship with your father. Are you ready if he should make any more mistakes? Have you opened your heart all the way?"

"I don't know for sure but I think he's ready to be a father. I hope he is, you know he is 35 years old. If he messes up, I'm kinda prepared for it if he does, because I know he hasn't been there this long, so I'm, you know, if he does I'm prepared for it. It's not going to shut me down totally. I'm not trying to let myself open up fully to him yet because he hasn't shown me that he's really ready. He says what he says but actions speak better than words. What you did in the past, you can't change but you can change if you wanted to and if you're going to."

"When are you going to the jail to see your dad?"

Her mother blurted out, "Just tell her why we haven't gone yet!"

"I have piercings. I don't want to take my piercings out. You gotta take them out when you go to prison. It has to heal first. Cause it hasn't healed then if you take it out for too long, it'll close, so I have to wait until it heals."

I found out that the piercing on her tongue was actually done by her *grandmother*. Her mother seemed excited by and approving of the whole practice. "They have piercings like you wouldn't believe! You wouldn't believe the things they're piercing. They have books you can look at and pick out anything you want."

Wanting to get back to the topic of her father, Natalie was quick to change the subject. "My dad went to court today so I want to write him and have him write me back letting me know what happened in court. When he's going to be moving to another prison. How long he's going to be gone."

"Nat, your father just wrote you a letter and it's on the dining room table at home," Maria informed her daughter. "In a letter he wrote to me he was bragging 'You're going to be my wife, we're going to be a family again.'" She shared these thoughts with me and her daughter as though the possibility was better than the alternative of living without him.

"Did you open mine?" Natalie asked her mother.

"They were together. It said my name and there was a letter for you and a letter for me. The letters were together. I didn't read yours. I read mine and put yours on the table. But everything he wrote to me was about you. 'My queen! My little queen! My little princess! When I get out I will tell you everything I did and we can start with a clean slate.'"

"He told me he wanted to get a tattoo of my face and then put daddy's little girl and my date of birth where everyone can see it," Natalie proudly pronounced her father's intent.

"What are your plans for the future?"

"My plan is to graduate and go to college for a police officer. My friend, her uncle is a police officer for the city. I went with him in the garages and they get the poor people, the bums, the homeless and they bring them to the Cadillac Hotel downtown. We went down there, we helped them, we told them 'Come on! Get up! We're going to take you to the Cadillac Hotel tonight!' We helped them get in the truck. We brought 'em down there. We handed out socks and gloves and stuff. Even food—like we packed little bags full of granola bars or the Nutri-Grain bars, stuff like that and gave it to each one of 'em. And we did it, we do loads, like when the bus is full we go drop them off and then we'll go back out. We find all the homeless people and we bring 'em to the hotel and we do it with two police officers in the van. There was a kid from college, then me, and my friend, two high school students, and an undercover behind us. Behind him we had the big truck that the homeless people go in. It was from 10:00 P.M. at night to 1:00 A.M. in the morning.

"But I'd like to do it. I want to be a police officer. Any kind. I'd be a police officer in the jail to watch prisoners. I'd ride around in the car. I'd do anything. I'd rather be in the correctional facility as a police officer working with prisoners.

"I put in a letter I wrote to my dad. I said, 'I hope when you get out you show me you're going to be a father.' I would really like that, to be able to have my real mom and my real dad. I've always wanted that, but I was never old enough to make that decision. 'I hope

I'll always be your little princess and that you could be here with me and mom. Even though you're not here now and haven't been, *I will always be your little queen. That's all.*' I've always wanted him to be around."

Natalie's mother walked me to the door and shared with me the reasons he was in jail and the fact that he may be there for a long time. The father plans on sharing his past mistakes with his daughter. I wonder if he is going to tell her that he was recently arrested for much more than drugs. I wonder how his daughter will feel about him when he shares with her, his princess, his little queen, his arrest for endangering the welfare of a child by raping a 13-year-old girl. Or the tattoo he wears proudly that defines him as a "Latin Lover." I wonder if he will tell her the other incidences of rape and criminal sexual activity he has been involved with. His violations of parole, burglary and drug charges have already been forgiven by his daughter. And I worry that her need to have a father in her life will prevent her from seeing the truth and shield her in a sense of denial about his heinous sexual crimes on girls younger than she.

For the Man (or Woman) Is the Product of the Child

His name is Simeon, and he's a 39-year-old African American male who has been incarcerated for 18 years of his life. Simeon is a big man both in height and weight with a bubbly personality to match. He has seven children by five different mothers. I interviewed him in the living room of the halfway house at which he had been ordered to reside for the first six months following his most recent release from prison. Simeon's story starts from the time he was a young child, when he was innocently known as "Miss Tessy's son."

"My mother was a street woman and I say that with the best of respect for her. She did all she could to take care of us. She was from the South, she didn't know no better. We became migrant workers picking oranges and apples and we worked our way to come to Rochester, got a city apartment, and got into the street life. My life became about prostitution and drugs. Like I say, I have stepsisters and stepbrothers and all them was into the street life in one way or the other. I've seen my mother 'turn dates'. My mother would give me liquor at the age of two, so that I would go to sleep so she could do what she had to do in order to turn dates. I've seen my sisters working at strip clubs. I was a 'mule' for a while, someone that moves drugs for people."

"Tell me about your first experience with prison."

"Well, I started not into the prison system, but I started in boys' homes at the age of 13, through the Parents Petition Program through Monroe County Courts. At the time, my mother was into gambling and some other stuff. My grandmother helped raise us and she would beat me, no matter whether I did anything wrong or not. She said if you thought it, it was a sin. So I got to be one of those kids, I'm gonna get beat when I get home anyway, so I might as well do what I want to do. My mother, she had her choice: me, or my brother. She gave me up and sent me to the home and let my other brother, that's in Alabama now, she kept him in for a lot of time. I had a lot of anger.

"My mother, like I say, she was a street woman. My father worked at a meat packing company. My mother met a guy and they fell in love while she was married to my father. She wanted a divorce so she could get with this other guy. My father didn't want to give her a divorce so, instead of giving her a divorce, he killed himself when I was seven years old. For a lot of years, I had a lot of hatred for women. My mother was such a street woman that at five years old I was going to the hospital because I had a full blown case of VD, and at five years old I was taking four shots of penicillin. I got the VD because my babysitter was steadily molesting me and raping me. I mean, life is just crazy, if you can understand what I'm saying. I'm Miss Tessy's son and you'll hear me say that a lot because I am Miss Tessy's son. She told me I'm raising men and you're my son and do whatever you feel and Miss Tessy was my mother and that's what I did. Miss Tessy's son didn't take 'No,' and I end up getting a conviction from that. I end up, I got a two-to-six for that. I went to jail for rape."

"How is your relationship with your children?"

"I'm going to keep it real. I'm not going to sit here and try to paint you no picture like I'm a good father. My kids can call me and say, 'Dad, I need this, I need that,' and if I'm able to or even if I'm not able to, I'm going to get that for them because I don't know how to be a father to them. I know how to give them things, if you under-stand what I'm saying, because my father was never there and my mother was really never there. I mean, in my heart, I want to be, but I was never there because I can't stand little kids crying. I can deal with the big part but the little kids crying, I'm not with that, like, 'Get your brats,' so I'll go onto the next woman and that's why I've got so many kids by so many different women."

"Tell me about them."

"My first child is a son, Jaron , he's 19, and he's by a woman named Malene. I thought she was all there but at the time, she was a street girl and I was into street women because of that lifestyle I came up with. I got with her, I'm doing my thing, I'm in clubs and she looked good under my arm but she was really a 'ho.' I hate those kinda words, excuse me. She was messing with me and a couple other guys. We moved in together and we got a son, Jaron. She already had five kids that her mother had custody of.

"The second child, Lesia, is from Lela. I had just went back to prison and had did a little bid for a couple months for drugs and driving, and was out again. So I went to be with Lela. Now Lela, she wasn't no good-looking female. She wasn't the kind of female that I was used to being around. She was ugly, but she was true to me and she really loved me. And I mean, talk about really loved me! I have never had a woman love me the way this woman loved me! I couldn't take Lela into the clubs with me, but she was really a good person.

"Then I met Tachell's mom, Ebony. I'm living with Lela and with Ebony. The next thing I know Lela pops up pregnant with twins, and we already had Lesia! A week later Ebony pops up pregnant and a couple days later Mishon pops up pregnant. I'm like, WOW! So there's all this popping. Ebony was the rape and I did eight years for that.

"Mishon had Tyrus. He's 18, and me and him have a relationship. I haven't seen him since I came home in May. I messed up our relationship before I went to jail this last time because he has images of his old dad, the drug dealer, the pimp, the hustler. Before I left I had gotten back into selling drugs and stuff, and I was doing some weed a couple of times. I'm trying to get him away from me because I'm trying to save him from being like me. I haven't seen him since I've been home, and he went through some stuff after I left; he got into some street stuff. What I'm saying, he's not built like that, he's not built to do what I did in the streets and take what I did. I came from a different lifestyle from what his mother made him come from.

"I'm going to tell you… my backbone, my whole life, has been Lela. Not only do we have a daughter, Lesia, we have a set of twins, Baron and Bevaun. All of them has been separated and different things since I was in jail and stuff when their mother passed away. Their mother passed away two days before Christmas. Two days before Christmas."

"Do you have a relationship with those three children?"

"Well, I have a relationship with Lesia. She just e-mailed me today, she's eighteen. She talks to her brothers and sisters, the twins, (they're sixteen) about me. I haven't been able to talk with them, they're mad at me because I'm in and out of the jail situation.

"My daughter Lesia, she came up from a caterpillar to a beautiful butterfly on her own. Her daddy was really never there, I was always in the streets. Her mother suffered from Lupus, if you know what that is. She had another medical problem that kept her sickly but Lesia, she just blossomed, Man! This girl is just . . . beautiful! She's phenomenal! I didn't know it either that she was raped. A lot of stuff's been coming at me since I been in this parenting class and I'm starting to learn how to communicate with them and find out stuff, and it's like, Whew! You just wouldn't believe it.

"Ebony's my only regret; she had my daughter Tachell with my two grandkids. Ebony's my only really regret because I got with her on a bet. I really didn't like her red southern behind. You know how men are about women. Who can get this one, who can get that one? I'm a mac, I can get this one. I really never loved Ebony. Even though Tachell wants to be in my life and I talked to Tachell, and I seen the grandkids a couple of weeks ago.

"Tachell, I'm going to be stuck with her because Tachell's me. Tachell comes from the ghetto. She is a high school drop out and she's what you would consider a 'ghetto hood rat.' She lives in the ghetto. She has my two grandkids and all she wants to do is smoke, drink and follow behind my footsteps. She's used to the ghetto and that's where her life is. She doesn't know what love is because she really has never experienced it. The streets is her love—not her children, my grandchildren—but the streets. She has a boy and a girl from two different men. She was 13, she got pregnant by this guy who had HIV, he was messing around with all the young girls here. At her age, as you look at her now she has always been well developed, big breasted, big butt. Her mother's big, I'm big. She never looked her age at thirteen.

"Then there's Siarah, and she has Jamarcus Odell Serique Abdul Umar. I have a relationship with Jamarcus, he's 5 years old."

"Do you ever see your grandchildren?"

"Yes, they're three and two, I think they are, or something like that. I'm not sure. I seen 'em. Thanks to Siarah, Jamarcus' mother, they stay around the corner from each other. Siarah wants to be with me and I would like to be with Siarah. She has Jamarcus and I would like to raise him.

"I talked to Tachell last week. I went over to Siarah's house. Tachell stopped over, gave me a hug and a kiss and tells me, 'Why you don't call me?' I said it's hard to get to this phone sometimes because it's like 10 guys in here. And I told her sometimes I don't want to deal with her attitude. Tachell's attitude is mean. She's straight-up ghetto, she's street, and she wants to do her way and that's the way I was.

"Nobody sees the change. All they see is the old Mac Daddy wanna-be player. Look at me, I got a hole in my neck, I got a scars over here, I got scoliosis, bad knees.

My ankles are tore. I'm gone. I'm almost 40. I'm blind. I'm wearing bifocals. I take over 13 pills a day. I gotta go for another operation in two months. This is my world.

"I want to tell you something from an African point of view, an African-American point of view; I want to say this right here. Black men, and I'm not using this for excuses, I don't never want anybody to think this is an excuse, but black men were never taught to be fathers. We were always taught how to go on the corners and brag about how many women we impregnated for the master and stuff, so most of us become that because we're never taught nothing else. I've been playing images, like I tell people, all my life; I've been a wanna-be something. I'm just now trying to find out who the hell I am, because as a black man, all's I ever wanted, six, seven women, a Cadillac and dice.

"Is your mother still alive?"

"No, she's dead and I know she went to hell. This woman, even when I came to the hospital shackled up—man! I seen this woman and I'm standing there looking at her and I'm like, to the day she died, the streets was in her. My mother died from drugs.

"Everybody in my family's been to jail, from my momma on down. My little sister, she'd get drunk every weekend, be it liquor and that weed. She acts like her momma and beat somebody up and she go to jail for it. She's 24 years old with five kids by five different fathers."

"How many brothers and sisters do you have?"

"My mother had five boys, four girls and she adopted a daughter. All of them have been in jail at some point or another. They all are junkies, drug addicts, or drunks. Nobody has escaped this."

"How about you?"

"I'm through. Man, I can't do it no more. I'm too old. I might look good at this age, almost 40, but I'm too old for this. I wear a back brace, knee brace, and ankle braces. I can't do no more. You know, I didn't love me and I've got to keep it real. For a lot of years, all I did was prostitutes. I didn't want a good woman like you. I wanted a prostitute. I wanted somebody that was slutty, nasty and grimy like me. I know, it sounds crazy! Like, wow!"

"What are you looking for now?"

"What am I looking for now? First of all, I want a god damn woman in my life. Somebody that loves God and loves God enough to be able to be honest with me and tell me, 'No! You messing up.' I don't believe that with the kind of credentials I have, the education I have, the skills I have, I have no business being at the bottom of the totem pole any more. I've learned something. Have you ever been to the park? If you ever go to the park, you'll see: pigeons pecking with pigeons eating their little seeds, the ducks hang with the ducks eating their little seeds, seagulls hang with the seagulls eating their little seeds, the hawks come down and they hang with the hawks when they take their little seeds, but you never see the pigeons and the ducks and the seagulls mix in. And I'm learning now birds of a feather flock together. If you want to be a winner, you got to be around winners. Nature will teach you some things if you really just look at nature. We might all be birds but we seem different kinds of birds. You'll find somewhere in life that you'll say, 'Man, that does make sense though.

"Look where I came from. I'm Miss Tessy's son. Street life tore my family up. What hurts me now, my kids is been molested, I was molested. I mean at five years old. The way my mother did my father, and the hatred I have for women. That's why I liked the prostitutes for so long. There's no commitment because I know she's a slut. That's the way I was and I don't like being there. I want something different out of life.

"Right now, and this might be crazy; my next woman could be 600 pounds with three strands of blond hair hanging down the front of her face, and orange lipstick. If a woman like that was going to treat me smart and make sure I'm on the right path, I'm in love! Not looks no more. Look at me. I got a hole in my throat; I got braces on my knee, I'm lucky to get anything. I really just want to have a relationship with Jesus so I can learn how. I want to learn this parenting thing so I can learn how to have a relationship with my kids."

Simeon arranged for me to interview his daughter, Tachell—his "ghetto girl." His driving directions led me to the worst part of the inner city. Upon entering the house I was surprised by the size of the rooms. I walked into the living room and was invited to sit on the sofa. A further observation revealed a dining room with only a hutch. A door in the living room was closed and later I could see it was a bedroom where her mother was. A bamboo covering blocked an archway where a friend lived. We sat in the living room where the walls were sparse; there were no pictures and no lamps. The sofa was filthy and the walls had never been cleaned.

Tachell is an African-American woman and like her father she is a very large woman. The clothes she wore were tight and dirty. The conversation was difficult to understand as she had an obvious speech impediment. Her daughter, age four, is a beautiful little girl with dozens of barrettes in her hair. I chatted with her for a few moments and then she sat by my side, staring at me throughout my entire interview with her mother.

"The first time my dad went to prison I was about three years old and at the time I lived with my mom. I remember he was there one minute and the next minute he was gone. When I was about nine years old he came home again. From what I remember when I was little, he use to be one of my favorite people but then I guess as we growed up from a tiny child to an older child it was like I went through changes, it's like I grew apart from him. I didn't know who he was; he didn't seem like the same person. I hadn't seen him in six or seven years and he can't tell me what to do; he haven't raised me. I was raised by my mother and that's who I listen to. So, we have a lot of differences. I feel mainly if he hadn't went to prison as many times as he did, we would have a better relationship than what we do now.

"He is trying to build a relationship, I mean he calls and he asks about the kids but I still feel hurt in a way. I missed out on something by him being locked up so long. I was 13 when I got pregnant, now I'm 18 with two kids; my daughter is four, and my son is three."

"Does your dad spend any time with the grandchildren?"

"He's seen them two or three times since he been out, but I don't feel comfortable with leaving my children around him. Now, if he's around awhile and I'm seeing them it's not a problem, but for me to leave my kids I wouldn't feel too comfortable. Even though you are my father I don't know what you're thinking about and I'm not going to leave my kids with just anybody, even though you have the label as my father. I just can't get up and say, 'Hey, I need you to watch the kids.' Then I was hearing stories about him that he was a rapist and a racist and a sex offender and stuff like that, and that's not the kind of stuff I want around my children. I'm not saying I made 110 percent of the right choices but it's just some things that I know is not right. I never sat down really and talked to him, and asked him was he a racist or sex offender. When the time is right I'll sit down and talk to him.

"I'm angry in a way but in a way not. I'm angry because I felt I was missing something but on the other hand I can't be angry because my mother was there for me for whatever I needed. So, I still had something there but it would have been nice to have him that was there.

"I'm *not* one of his favorite children; I already know that. I was told not to hold my tongue for nobody so I guess if he makes me mad I tell him exactly how I feel. I'm not going to sugarcoat it and make it nice. I have no father, I mean I have a father 'cause somebody had to get my mom pregnant but as really having a father— *I don't have no father.* I know I make him feel bad sometime the way I talk to him but that's just me. I can't help what I do, I can probably change for the better, but right now I don't see myself changing towards him. We gonna have to build more of a whole relationship, as if I was an infant."

"Do you want to build a relationship with your father?"

"In a way, yes and in a way no. I don't want to force nothing on him that he doesn't want. But in the same way of thinking I would like to know him before it was to happen to any one of us, like, to be dead. I'd like to say, he use to do this or I use to do this with him, or we use to do this together and right now I can't say that."

"I told people I don't have a father. My mother use to tell everybody he was in jail, he was in prison. She told me, he love you, but I felt if you're not here with me, so you don't love me."

"Did the children at school ask you where your dad was?"

"It wasn't really an issue, it wasn't something that really came up, but when it did I answered it truthfully. I would say he's locked up and I don't have a father, because I felt if he would have loved me he wouldn't had been where he was at. Then, when he was out, I was about eight or nine, we tried to build a relationship. It was so hard because he wanted to do what he wanted to do. I didn't like it at all because my mother tried to force me up on him when he got out of prison. My mother use to make me spend the night with him, get to know him and I didn't want to.

"I never really had a father, it was either jail or streets, jail or streets, jail or street; and either way it goes, one of them was more important then me and it seemed to always be, jail or streets."

"Do you think he'll end up back in prison again?"

"I honestly can't say 'cause it seems like every time he goes to jail or prison whatever he do, he goes one way and he comes back another way. He comes out and he'll be going to church and he'll be doing this and that and doing good for himself. Then sooner or later he's back out on the streets doing whatever he does, and that's what lands him right back to jail. He's been in and out of jail for about 18 years."

This next story also took me to one of the worst parts of the inner city of Rochester, New York, in search of Simeon's girlfriend, Siarah. When I arrived at her home,

Siarah—a very large black woman—answered the door and welcomed me inside. The house was decorated with numerous pictures of children and family. Siarah introduced me to her children, Jamarcus, age five, and her daughter, Aysha. At five years old, Jamarcus was 115 pounds and Aysha was also an obese young lady. As I talked with the five-year-old I was crushed to hear him speak. He was unintelligible. Siarah could tell I wasn't able to understand him and translated his comments. Aysha also spoke in a way that was simply too difficult to understand. During the course of the interview the children silently watched television and ate.

"Simeon has been to jail several times; this is just the last one I hope. Two-and-a-half years ago he went to prison; Jamarcus was two when he went. He went because he had a drug addiction problem. We were living together at the time but then he worked it out to leave, and disturbed the house. My son didn't know where his father was and why he wasn't home with us.

"It was very difficult for us because we're use to having him around. We went up to visit, of course, a few times to visit him in the county jail, which is here in town. It wasn't very pleasant to visit him there because he didn't make it easy for us at all. When he went up-state, I didn't go up there to visit as much, I might of went up there two of three times when he first went in.

"He was up-state, in Groveland Correctional Facility, and they didn't make it too comfortable when we went up to see him. We went through a lot of harassments; you went through having to take off your clothes and if you had wire in your bras you had to take it out. People in there were very nasty and by the time you got to the visit you were already in an uproar because of going through everything you had to go through to get in there. It wasn't as easy to travel even though it was close to us; especially when weather was bad, so I didn't visit him too much when he went up-state.

"I didn't like the whole jail scene 'cause it felt like I was being a prisoner. I didn't like the visits; he was always stressed out about one thing or another. Financially, I could not help him out because I didn't have the money to send him 'cause I had to take care of my kids. Jamarcus couldn't understand why his dad wasn't around because he knew he always seen his sister's dad, Jomo, but not his dad. It was very hard to explain to him that he didn't have a lot of things. You have to get up to the prison on your own so you know that chaoticness. I wasn't with it, that's why I didn't got up there to see him too much.

"For one, they don't make it comfortable for children to be up there. When kids are up there they have to sit in their seats, and how many four- or five-year-olds are just gonna sit down for a visit for any amount of time, and if it's more than an hour, it ain't happening. The prison guards tell you that they have a play area for the kids but then it's like, the kids can be playing, but if they don't have anyone to supervise the play area, then they have to shut it down. If the children are playing and the prisoner who is guarding the play area has to go back to his cell, then the kids have to sit down. That's why I said I felt that I was a prisoner. There wasn't a lot of things that I could do as far as anyone helping me out. As far as getting out there, as far as finding rules and regulations, they say they gave a book to the inmates. I would like to have a book on my own 'cause I would like to know what is being said or what can you do, or what can't you do. So you know, the guards were not very good with directions; they were not very good with rules and regulations and when they did tell you they were very nasty.

"The prison had a conference area where the prisoners could buy their things, but the things was outrageous in prices for them to be able to buy things. You can buy one bar of soap and pay one dollar or more and that's kind of expensive when you're in prison so a lot times it would be cheaper for me to send it. When you send things, it don't always get there, or gets there broke or they search through things so much and take out what they want to give you, or what they don't want you to have and then you got to worry about getting the box sent back to you through the mail. That was hard because once it got sent back, you didn't know when it was gonna get sent back and it could come back, to you in any condition and they didn't care and they weren't taking blame."

"Did you take Jamarcus to the prison to visit his father?"

"Yes, I took Jamarcus up about eight times, but only three times up-state. I took him mostly when he was right here in the county jail. Going upstate I had did that with my daughter with my…Well, with my soon-to-be ex-husband and I just felt that it was taking away from her childhood."

"Can you tell me what the visit was like?"

"You got to get up, go, and then you never know what kind of mood he's in when you go. The guards treat anybody nasty, they treat kids nasty, adults nasty, and I just didn't want to take them through that experience. That's why I didn't push the issue of taking him too much 'cause I didn't like the way they talked to me, let alone the way they were talking to my son. At the time, when I was taking him he was only between three going on four and they were not very nice to him."

"What were the visits like for Jamarcus?"

"Well, when we went up he would, of course, talk to his dad for a little, 'cause he was glad to see him, and then they had a play area where they could go. He would play in there and they had toys and you could watch TV. But then I found that the few times I did take him up there he would be in the play area playing and we may have been there a half hour. Then the guards would say, 'Oh well, we got to shut the play area down because the inmate who's attending the area has to go back to his cell.' 'Okay, ya'll don't have another inmate to come in!' That made me very frustrated because you know how kids are, they're playing and you take something they're playing with, or something that's keepings their attention, if you just take it, which means: no if, ands, buts about it. He had a fit! Jamarcus then came over to the table and sat with us but what kid wants to just sit? Even though he was glad to see his dad, and excited to be up there with him, but the point is, he didn't have anything to do. The guards would just close it down *anytime.*

"Then there's the lock-down. There was only certain times you can leave the visit and if you didn't leave at that certain time you were locked in until after the count of the prisoners was over. The count is at 2:00 P.M. and they wouldn't let any movement go on from 2:00 P.M. until the visit was over, which was at 3:30 P.M., so therefore, we got locked in there from two o'clock. Let's say they do the count and then they close up the kids section; then he has to sit there for a whole hour and a half, they can't do anything but just sit there."

"What is it like for Jamarcus not having his father around?"

"Oh, it was very strainful for him 'cause he was in school and they have what they call a father/son thing at his school. He didn't have his dad around, 'Mommy but my dad's not here and everybody else's dad is.' I had to explain to him that he was gone away. And, at first I didn't tell him his dad was in jail, I just tell him he was gone away. He figured he was always home, but I don't know how it came about. In the file, they have a section where they write where your daddy's "incarcerated" so maybe somebody said something to him. Maybe he could have overheard me talking but he found out he was in prison, and it was really hard. I knew other kids had their dads and I would still take him to the father/son program; y'know, but everybody's with their dad.

"Well, I said, Jamarcus, your dad can't be here 'cause where he is... and I just tried to explain it to him the best I could. He never really fully understood why he couldn't be there, y'know, and it made him feel bad. When some of the kids' parents weren't around their kids would say things like 'Yeah, your dad's not here and mines is.' He talked about his dad all the time; he missed him. He had a problem dealing with that and he talked about it the whole school year. It was a strain on him 'cause a lot of the dads came up to the school and did a lot of things. They volunteered for the school and he never understood quite fully why his dad wasn't here, so all I could do was explain it to him the best I could. I think he had a lot of disappointment 'cause he would see my daughter go with her father. 'Why can't I go to my dad's house?' He would always ask. That's what he called the jail, his dads house, 'cause that's all he knew. Jamarcus kept asking me, 'I want to go see him,' but we just don't have the money. My car wasn't working some of the time and I said I just couldn't go up there."

"Did Simeon call you from the jail?"

"I can't afford to have my phone bill run up and sometime when things got stressful for Simeon in jail, he would call, call, call, so I blocked it myself. I can't afford it. Then, when my husband, Jomo, my daughter's father, would call . . . I can't afford this."

Simeon and Siarah were never married. The man she is married to now is her daughter's father, whom she met while Simeon was in jail. She was a little embarrassed at her life.

"Yeah, I did, I did, that was an awful wrong mistake. That's been over 10 . . . we've been married almost 11 years now, but we've been separated most of that time 'cause we were only together six months after he go out of prison.

"I was at that jail like it was a job. On Saturdays and Sundays, I was at that jail from eight o'clock in the morning until nine-thirty at night, didn't get home until 10:30 P.M.. That's why I didn't go much with Simeon 'cause I had learned from that experience from my husband. I couldn't take my kids through that 'cause it's just very strainful. It might have not been as hard on me but for the kids it is, because they don't make it enjoyable. They don't make you feel comfortable in there."

"Now that Simeon is out of prison how is the relationship between Jamarcus and his father?"

"Jamarcus was glad when his dad came home because then he could tell everybody, 'This is my dad!' I mean, as soon as he came home we took him to the school because he wanted everybody to see his daddy. He talked with his teachers all the time about his father; he talked about him coming home. 'I want my dad home,' he would tell me. I would tell him he has to stay in there for the things he did that wasn't right. You have to kinda wait, so when his dad got out he had to explain to him why he was in jail and that it wasn't a good place and he should never want to go there. Still today he can't understand why his dad doesn't live here because once he came home he figured he would live with us. Now that he's staying at the halfway house he can't understand why. I didn't even think about it until he came home to even explain the fact that he wouldn't be living with us. I told him, 'because that's what happens when a person comes out of jail they have to stay somewhere for awhile.'

"Jamarcus still has a problem with him not coming here even when we take him back to the halfway house. 'Why does he have to go there?' I have to explain to him he has to stay in his house and we have to stay in our house. When we get married then we can move together. If that's not happening then daddy will come and visit as much as he can, 'See, we can't go where he lives, we can't visit there.'"

"Does he have the ability to spend the time here at the house with all of you?"

"Only when he gets special passes they give him every other weekend. He stays from Friday to Sunday, and he just had one last weekend. He stayed here, 'cause parole and everything has to know where he's staying and he still has to remember no matter where he's staying his curfew is still nine o'clock."

"What do Jamarcus and his father do when they are together for the weekend?"

"Usually they go up to the playground, he colors with him, and they watch movies, go sit in the room and read books, talk. They have problems having to give Simeon respect; that's because Simeon basically been gone the majority of his life. When Jamarcus was first born he wasn't around because of his addiction; he was out getting high. Then when he came back from that, he got help and went to rehab.

"Jamarcus hasn't been around him long enough to know that he has to listen and respect him. As far as Jamarcus is concerned, he knows it's his dad. Simeon feels he's not giving him any respect so he clashes with that, and that's gonna take time. All Jamarcus knows is my mom's been here and that's the only person I know. I tell Simeon, I don't feel like beating him is going to teach him, you got to first build a bond. He's like, 'Well, I do stuff with him,' and I said, 'Yeah, you got to keep on doing that because you can't just stop 'cause he's being disrespectful or because he's talking back or not listening.' Right now Jamarcus don't know if his daddy's staying here or not. He will say to me, 'Well, Mom, how long is Daddy going to be out? Is he going back to jail, when he going back to jail?'"

"How is Jamarcus doing at school?"

"Jamarcus, he does excellent in school; he's one of the top kids in his school. He's very bright, he gets excellent reports from school. He gets along with everybody. He does his work, he's working on some things above his average. They are recommending me to get him into a very exceptional school because he's so bright. He's very outgoing, very talkative."

"The teachers would tell me how he always talked about his dad. That was one of the reasons why I explained to them, 'cause I don't know if they look at his records or not, but it's in there that he was incarcerated. I got him into one of the top schools here. I didn't know if I was going to be able to get him in, but two days ago I got the letter and he got accepted in and that's the 'magnet program.' That's for high standard students for kids that are smart. The school usually puts kids wherever and usually in their neighborhood. This is not the best neighborhood, I don't like this neighborhood, but I have to live here for certain circumstances because I'm on Section 8."

"Does Jamarcus have any problems with school?"

"No problems as far as school, he had speech problems but they never actually said it was a speech problem. The school never suggested I put him in speech classes, it just said to be worry of that 'cause in certain words the ending didn't come out because of the missing teeth. I understand everything he says, but some people may not if they're not use to his talking. To me he talks clear, but she said it's something to be aware, 'cause once the teeth grow in if he's still having a problem, then that was a concern. The school is not recommending him for speech and he never had to go through any counseling or anything."

"Does Simeon call Jamarcus now that he's in town and it doesn't cost long distance fees?"

"Oh yeah, he calls him at night, he calls him in the mornings. When he was in school he'd call him before school and when I go pick him up from school he calls on my cell phone. When he got home he called and then he would call before he goes to bed.

"Simeon tries to do all he can since he's been home. He's bought my son maybe 16 pair of pants and took the time to cut and hem them 'cause they're a 36 waist. Even with the shirts 'cause the shirts are always way down to his knees because of his size Simeon cuts them off. He's so short, I can buy a pair of shorts with a 36 inch waist and they're pants on him. They're still not all the way down, so they look like high waters. I have him wear those as shorts and because he's getting taller now the shorts are now starting to look like shorts and not pants anymore. It's very expensive to buy these clothes 'cause you can't just go anywhere you can't just go to Wal-Mart.

"Because I have to buy for two kids, money is tight 'cause I'm on a fixed income, I'm on SSD and SSI 'cause I'm disabled. I got hurt on my job so therefore Simeon's trying to do as much as he can for them. Anytime he can get a little bit of money—he went this week and got them both sneakers for school."

"How is Simeon's relationship with your daughter?"

"My daughter, me and Simeon been around since she's been born, he treats her like she is his and that's the only really father figure she knows. Simeon is the only man she stands up for. She gave him a lot of problems, but that's the only person that's ever done stuff with her. He's tooken her to the parks, he's tooken her to movies, he did sit up and did arts and crafts with her. He does everything with her, and that's the only person she's really attached to. She's not even attached to her own dad like she is to Simeon because her daddy's not around. He does nothing, he doesn't keep it real. Simeon takes a lot of time, he does things for her that no other man I've ever been with ever did, and that's been since she's been born. She's 15 now, so that's the only really father figure she knows. She gives him a hard time sometime and she knows he loves her.

"She's even having a bad time with him in jail 'cause they're so close she doesn't say it, but I just feel as though she's very angry. She asks him, 'When you gonna stay out of jail?'"

Aysha realized we were talking about her and came over to join in on the conversation. "Your mom tells me you have a wonderful relationship with Simeon?" She mumbled some words and her mom realized I couldn't understand what was just said so the mother had to translate.

"She said, 'He thinks that she's mean to him but she's not.'"

With probing the young girl managed to mumble out, "I love him. He takes me on picnics and stuff. On my birthday, my mom didn't have no money to take me and do nothing so I guess he won some tickets to a game and gave them to me."

Siarah explains, "Simeon knew I couldn't afford it and he knew she wanted to go and he sat up and listened to the radio and he called in and I think it was the 11th caller or something but he gave her the tickets. But the thing is, he had other kids that he could have gave them to, but he gave them to her. I mean, we get mad at him sometimes 'cause he does stuff that he has no business doing, but I know he has our best interest at heart. Simeon is a good person. I figure if he just stays off of drugs he'll stay out of prison. There's not nothing I wouldn't do for him 'cause I know there's not nothing he wouldn't do for me."

Through some of the parenting classes he attends, Simeon learned of the devastating impact his bad choices have made on his children. He has learned of the children's sacrifice when they spend weekends in a prison environment that makes it perfectly clear they are not welcomed. He has learned the choices he's made leave his children ever wondering, ever worrying if he is going to be there for them. It is this author's hope that Miss Tessy's son has the courage to stop the pain.

Postscript: Shortly after I completed the interviews for this story, I learned that Simeon passed away. He had recently moved out of the halfway house and into his own apartment. Simeon was found on a couch with a writing pad in his hand. The final words he had written were, "I'm free now."

My Mom's at College

T HE SCHOOL WAS ABUZZ with the news that Catrina's mother was arrested for embezzling money from her employer. The articles in the paper were brief and did not give much information. On the other hand, like most small towns, Rochester had a narrow-minded mentality when it came to situations like this—especially seeing as how it was a woman who was arrested.

I tried to stay somewhat removed from the situation, involved but not engulfed. In hindsight, I probably should have paid more attention to the goings-on instead of waiting until it hit me square in the face. I was walking through my building one morning, going in and out of classrooms while trying to keep a pulse on what was happening. Suddenly I opened the door to one room only to discover Catrina standing in front of her first-grade class sharing a story with the other children.

At six years old, Catrina is one of those little girls who unfortunately always appears a bit disheveled. Her long hair, pulled on top of her head, is black like a stallion's mane and looks just as wild, her eyes as dark as her hair. Her clothes, while cute on a certain level, just don't seem to work together, and never seem to be very clean.

"The police officer picked us up in a bus," I heard her say, "and we went and picked out some toys. My mother couldn't go with us because she was at college."

Catrina was actually referring to "Shop with a Cop," a program sponsored by the local police department. The police contact the school requesting children with high needs, and the school chooses two children whose families would benefit from Christmas presents. The children meet at a local restaurant for lunch and then take a bus to Wal-Mart or K-Mart where they shop for the whole family. They later return to the restaurant for their families to pick them up.

When she's on her medication for ADHD, and the medication is working correctly, Catrina is a student who excels in her class. She is monitored closely by her teacher since she once went through a series of reactions to the medication which included being withdrawn and completely shut down from the learning process at school. Our concerns rose even higher when she said to us, "I don't want to live any more."

We also learned through discussions with her father that she was watching television late into the evening. With the television removed from the bedroom and Catrina in bed by 8:00 P.M., there has been a remarkable difference in her academic performance at school. Her expression and innerself pour out in her writing and in illustrations which are truly remarkable for a first-grader—especially considering the fact that she is not an expressive child on a verbal level. Her writings and illustrations have enabled us to delve into her psychological make-up, and try to understand what she is feeling on an ongoing basis.

Usually, when I see children in the hall, they run up and give me a hug or wave so hard that their hand is like a helicopter propeller ready to lift them to the sky! Their faces glow and their smiles spread from ear to ear. Even when they are hurrying to their classrooms they never fail to wave and say "Hi, Ms. Martone!" But never Catrina. With her, it's like watching a child who is detached and in a world of despair.

Catrina's father comes into the school quite often, and that afternoon I called him into my office to talk with him. He typically doesn't like visiting me in my office; he always tells me that it makes him nervous to meet with the school principal. And yet, Mike is the type of person who is always upbeat and easygoing. He stands about six feet tall and is always dressed in shorts—even during the depths of winter. His black hair is cut in military style, cropped close to the head. He also always wears short sleeve shirts that show off the tattoo of a bear on his lower arm. I never see him without his gold cross around his neck, and was not surprised to learn from him that he had a deep faith.

"I couldn't do it without Him, Cynthia. Everything I'm going through and all the help I'm getting . . . You know, it is really hard, I love her and hate her at the same time. I know she did it to help me out with the other problems . . ." his voice trailed off. "Without her money, we had to move to a place we don't really like and I had to get on food stamps. I'm used to having a home but I couldn't afford it with what I make alone. The three of us are crammed into this tiny apartment. I can't play my music without one of my neighbors complaining. My two girls share the bedroom and I sleep on the couch."

I offered my support to him, the resources of the school and Catrina's teachers, and then suggested it might be helpful if I went with him and the girls to visit their mother in prison.

"Ms. Martone, it is not really a place I think you will like."

His concern for me was admirable, yet, I could sense that deep down he wanted me to go. He wanted all the support and help he could get. I had no doubt that raising three children alone was a daunting task. After trying a few times to set up a date, we were finally able to arrange a time when I would take him and the children to the prison for a visit. He gave me directions to his apartment complex and asked me several times if I was sure I wanted to go. The night before our scheduled prison visit Mike called me.

"Cynthia," he said in a sheepish voice. "I need to tell you something but I'm a little uncomfortable." He kept pausing. "I'm really not sure how to tell you this. Visiting the prison is such a degrading thing. You are so classy and so above this. Are you really sure you want to spend the day there?"

"Just tell me, I'm sure it is nothing that will be new to me." I assured him.

Sheepishly, and with a great deal of hesitation in his voice, he continued, "If you wear an under-wire bra the alarm will go off and the guards will make you take it off and put it in a bag."

"I'm so glad you told me!" I laughed. "Thank heavens I know now. Not a problem and I know what I'll do. I simply will not wear one! I'll see you in the morning and everything will be fine. It will be a good day."

He thanked me profusely and hung up the phone.

It was bitter cold the following morning and it took the car forever to warm up. I arrived at the family's apartment at 7:00 A.M.; Mike and his two daughters must have been waiting for me because they came out as soon as I arrived. The girls were dressed in pretty pink coats and scarves. I could barely see their faces; only their eyes peeked through the scarves and hats. They all looked very tired, with dark circles under their eyes. Getting up at 6:00 A.M. is a bit difficult for children. Their dad strapped them in the seat belts and off we went for the 90-minute drive to the prison. There was no noise from the back seat, but Mike had plenty to say.

"It is so hard getting these girls up in the morning. They are constantly fighting with each other. This is a lot of work, and I go through this every week. I'm so tired." Mike told me that their system for visitation was an alternating one: Mike and the girls would visit one week on Sunday and the next week on a Saturday.

On our way to the prison we stopped at a gas station for coffee and juice. I was a little taken aback when Mike mentioned that he had to buy seven packs of cigarettes at seven dollars a pack. It surprised me since I knew their financial situation was extremely tight. How could so much money be spent on cigarettes? He must have read my mind.

"If I don't bring her the cigarettes she makes my life miserable and the visit is really bad. It just isn't worth it. She needs enough for the week so I buy her seven packs and bring them to her every week." He shared the information as though justifying his wife's fifty-dollar-a-week habit.

With some juice in their tummies, the girls began to come out of their slumber. Beth, the four year old, resembled Catrina, except that she had short hair. Being a very quiet child, she didn't say a word—she just smiled constantly, a big grin spread across her face. Catrina, on the other hand, had much to say as she talked about cleaning house and who was responsible for doing which chores.

"Catrina is a good cleaner. She makes the floors shine and she does all the laundry and dishes," her father proudly exclaimed.

"Beth, what do you do?" I asked.

"Nothing," Catrina blurted out for her sister.

I was surprised when Beth broke her silence and blurted out, "Yeah! I don't do anything."

About 90 minutes later we arrived at the Albion Correctional Facility. The building reminded me of those you see in the south: long and stately in red brick with white trim; quite a sight as you pull into the parking lot. It's such a shame to surround a beautiful building with silver barbed-wire that has an eerie glow because of all the ice beads frozen to the metal. All I could think about were the concentration camps I had seen in Germany. Mike's worrying about taking me along was at its peak and became even more intense as we got out of the car. Comforting him didn't seem to be working. He wasn't hearing my appreciation for how much I could learn from the visit.

"Cynthia, I feel really worried about you doing this and going in there. Are you sure? It is a whole day." His voice was torn with concern on one hand and wanting me to go on the other.

"Mike, I'm fine and really think it is a little late to be worrying about that now!" I replied, trying to make light of the situation.

We entered a processing place; to the right was an office behind a glass case with a slide-through panel much like you would see at money-exchange stations. There were tiny holes in the glass to speak into. Off to the left were a metal detector and a guard standing by it checking visitors as they passed through. To the left of the metal detector was a table. We had to fill out visitors' forms and have our IDs ready to show the guard before we walked through the metal detector. Mike put the cigarettes he brought his wife into a brown bag and wrote her name and prison number on the outside.

"The guards will give her the stuff after they check it out," Mike informed me.

There were several chairs, lockers, and a drinking fountain against the back wall. Except for my coat, I was not allowed to take anything with me into the visitation room; it had to go into the lockers. If the girls wanted to make anything for their mother they had to mail it to her. The expression of appreciation shown by a mother who has just been given a hand-made gift from her daughters would not be experienced by these children.

The line was moving very slowly. "I've never seen it like this. Usually we can walk right in and go on through," Mike commented.

I just nodded and smiled. "Not a problem."

After walking around the small room, the girls took their jackets off and left them on the chair. They got drinks from the drinking fountain and chatted to each other as they sat on the chairs. Beth kept coming up to me and would just smile with her huge grin, then go back and talk to her sister. The line was moving very slowly.

A black man in front of me kept mumbling, "What the fuck with this line?" He looked at me and out of the blue said, "If she thinks I'm going to do this fucking shit every weekend she is wrong! I don't have time to do this shit every week. This is bullshit." I didn't respond. I just thought to myself, *turn around, stop talking to me and quit using that filthy language in front of me and the children.*

I saw women coming out of the bathroom with their bras in hand, rolling their eyes in an attempt to commiserate with me. Others were complaining about the line and how much time it was taking to go through the metal detector. Everyone seemed so miserable and disgusted about having to be there. Yet the girls continued to sit in their chairs, unfazed by their surroundings, quietly talking to each other.

There were three black women ahead of us in the line. Once they passed through the metal detector the guard behind the glass started making rude comments after one of the women told the guard they needed to put their bras back on. He reminded me of a southern redneck with wide spaces between his teeth and a dirty grin from ear to ear.

Mike came up and whispered to me, "They take the bus up from New York City every week to visit their pimp girlfriend." The one woman was older, and the other two very young, I suspected in their twenties. The two young women wore clothes like those you would find in the Frederick's of Hollywood catalog. One by one I watched them go into the bathroom. Why didn't they eliminate all of this hassle and wear a bra that had no under-wire?! When it was time for them to go through the metal detector they took off their coats and handed them to the guard so he could hand inspect them.

"What's in the bag?" The guard asked. "My bra." The older woman commented as she pulled it out and dangled it in front of his face. I looked over at the girls and could see Catrina watching and listening to everything that was said and done.

A young woman with a baby showed up and sat quietly on a chair. I couldn't help but stare, or imagine having to expose my grandson to this environment. When I asked her the child's age, I learned he was only nine months old. I don't know what I would do if I were in this situation. She also told me that the baby's mother was in prison for robbery. They ended up sitting at the table next to us for the entire visit. This child, at the most critical time of his life, did not have his mother to nurture him, to love him, to bond with him. I wished I could see into the future and know what would become of him.

An hour passed and we were still only in the waiting area. "They are mean here; they treat you like you are nothing. I didn't commit any crime and shouldn't have to be treated or talked to the way they do. Watch when we go inside how mean the guards get." Mike's voice was a little loud. I didn't think it was a good idea to make statements such as those and agitate the guards. My motioning him to speak softly fell on deaf ears.

All the while, the girls were just watching and listening to everything that was going on. I could see Beth talking and laughing to Catrina, but Catrina contained her emotion as she always does. She is six years old, going on thirty-six. She will never get to experience a normal childhood. There is only time for work and being the "head" of the household, a mother to her sister.

The line was getting shorter now and Mike called the girls to get ready to walk through the metal detector.

Together, Mike and I gathered their things. They too had to take their boots off and Catrina, who must have learned from experience, took her belt off as well.

"Catrina, you didn't have to take your belt or your boots off," her father snapped in an agitated voice.

"Yes, I did," she replied to her father as though she knew more than he did; her tone sounded as though she were an adult.

I decided to hurry and take my boots off so as not to set off the alarm. Thank God Mike told me the night before about under-wire bras setting off the alarm! The girls walked through as though it was second nature and we followed behind. On the other side of the detector we had to give our paperwork to the guard. We were then buzzed into another holding area. Once there, we were once again buzzed into yet another holding area that led into an outdoor cage. They held us in the cage for a bit and I began to feel like some sort of animal. I wondered what was taking them so long to let us out. Plus, it was freezing! Perhaps Mike's assessment of the guards was correct. Finally, the sound of a buzz let us pass to the walkway that led to the main building.

Upon entering the visiting room, a guard area was immediately to our left and the tables for the visitors and prisoners to our right. The guards gave us a table number where we went and placed our coats. A short distance off to the left, where the guards sat, were the vending machines and a microwave oven. We all immediately headed over to the vending machines to get something to eat.

"I want milk." Beth announced.

"Me too, and can I get a Pop Tart?" Catrina blurted.

"I want pretzels, B7," Beth proudly announced, showing us she knew her numbers and letters.

"What would you like Cynthia?" Mike asked.

"Hot cocoa would be fine."

Mike finished buying more things for him and his wife. While he was busy doing that I noticed a children's room and asked the guard if I could take a look inside. Despite the sign that clearly stated, "No Adults," the guard nodded "yes," and I entered the room. I was curious as to what was available for the children since it was a long day to arrive at 8:00 A.M. and not be able to leave until 2:30 P.M. The room had shelves filled with games and toys and a metal locker was filled with even more items. There was a small teepee, a television with a VCR, child-size tables and chairs, and a carpet for the children to play on.

A black female prisoner who looked old and drawn with an expression of despair seemed to be in charge of taking care of the room. The girls followed me in and grabbed some crayons and paper. The woman never moved... she sat there with no emotion, not even a "hello" to the girls and only a nod to me. She just watched with a blank look on her face. I watched the girls as they rummaged through the shelves filled with supplies and chatted with each other about the crayon colors they wanted. I decided to leave them and go back to the table to be with Mike, thanking the guard on my way past for allowing me to enter the children's room and look around.

"This is what I do every week," Mike said to me as I rejoined him. "We never miss a week. There is one guard that is bad; she is not here today. She doesn't let you do anything, hold hands, nothing. I don't understand why she has to be so mean." It was too bad there wasn't a happy medium that could be reached. At Attica, what the children saw and heard bordered on the pornographic, and yet at this prison it was too much the opposite.

The girls came back to the table with their paper and crayons. Beth was feeling a little more comfortable with me and pulled up a chair right next to me. She didn't say anything, just smiled her big grin, while Catrina sat quietly and began to draw. Still no emotion, and only that despairing look.

"The wait is long for her to get here from the time she is called, usually 30 minutes. Are you girls still hungry?" He asked.

"Yes!" they both screamed out in unison.

We opened a bag of pretzels and Pop Tarts and started nibbling while we waited for their mom. One by one the female prisoners came through the door, walking the length of the room and down to the opposite end where the guards watched over the proceedings.

Finally, their mom entered the room. Deb was short and a little on the heavy side with bleached blonde hair with pitch black re-growth pulled into a ponytail. All the women had to wear their hair up and back off their necks—another security precaution. She wore a royal-blue sweater with her prison-issued green pants. Deb walked past the table, smiled slightly and nodded as she continued to go to the booth where the guards had to check her in. The prisoners were not permitted to say anything during the walk. When she was finally able to walk to our table, Beth hopped out of her chair and jumped into her mother's arms.

"I missed you!" Beth said, her arms tightly wrapped around her mother's neck.

Catrina didn't move, nor did she lift her head from coloring. I was so surprised by her reaction to seeing her mother. No emotion and no response; she just sat there and continued to draw. I so wanted to know what she was feeling and thinking.

"Catrina, don't I get a hello or a hug?" Deb asked her daughter.

"Hi," Catrina responded in a muffled voice that sounded as though she saw her mother every day. A few moments later she got up and gave her a hug and a kiss. It was a hug and a kiss that you would give someone you're forced to greet in that manner, not someone who you miss and love dearly. I never would have suspected that Catrina would behave in this manner.

"Hello, Cynthia, nice to see you," Deb said as she shook my hand. I thanked her for allowing me to come up for a visit. She leaned closer to me and whispered, "You do know that I'm in college?" Looking at me to ensure that I would go along with this charade. Against my gut, I nodded yes. I knew her mother and father had been telling the girls that she was away at college.

It had really shocked us at the school when Catrina shared with us that she never wanted to go to college. We begged Mike to talk to the counselor about what was being told to the girls. I don't believe in lying to children, especially when circumstances are so blatant. Mike and Deb have since changed what they tell their children; now, they say, Deb is at art school.

Throughout the course of the year, Catrina also shared with us that she didn't like to go to the counselor because the counselor tells her dad everything that is going on and then he yells at her. As a result, Catrina told us that she lies to the counselor by telling her that everything is all right. Mike and his daughter do not have a good relationship; from conversations we've had he seems to favor Beth, while he and Catrina simply clash.

It was now 10:00 A.M., and I felt as though I had been there for much longer. The room was starting to fill up with prisoners and their guests, and the noise level was rising.

"How is everything going in school? Are you doing all of your homework?" Deb asked Catrina.

Catrina only responded with "Okay," and a shrug of her shoulders. The questioning continued as Deb asked Mike how her sister was doing. He never failed to comment that his sister-in-law drove him crazy! Her expectations for what should be done with and for the girls are high and to listen to Mike she is very demanding of him. Deb's sister is instrumental in supporting the girls and Mike. She takes an interest in them as though they were hers, and is truly their fairy godmother. She comes to the school to pick Catrina up or take her to a doctor's appointment and she is there for Catrina's school events. When Catrina won an award it was her aunt who brought her to the ceremony, it was her aunt who took all the photos and fussed over how awesome it was to be there. Mike never came to the ceremony. I remember asking Catrina to smile for the camera and her reply was, "I really don't like to smile." And she never does. Her aunt even accepts the phone calls from her sister so that the girls can talk to their mother. Mike had shared with me that the phone bills were so high his phone was disconnected until the bill was paid.

Children of prisoners pay a high price for a loving phone call from their incarcerated parent. Local calls are $1.67 for the first minute; 9 cents a minute for the remainder of the call. The maximum charge for a local 15-minute call is $2.93. Long distance calls are $4.84 for the first minute; 89 cents per minute for the remainder of the call. The maximum charge for a 15-minute long distance call is $17.30. There is no access to e-mail. The old-fashioned way of corresponding by letter writing is the only viable method and the most cost effective.

The girls went off to the playroom and came back with some books and playing cards. Catrina read to all of us as her mother turned the pages and helped with some of the harder words. At the end of each page Catrina would look up at me with those puppy dog eyes waiting for my approval. I winked at her each time; she wouldn't start the next page until I did.

Beth pulled up her chair until it was touching mine and played cards by herself. Mike went off to buy his wife some milk, which she wasn't able to get enough of in the prison. He brought back some sandwiches and snacks for everyone to eat. The cost of the food is typical of vending machine prices: expensive. I had no doubt that it was easy to spend 20 dollars or more on food during each visit. Between the drive up and back, the cost of cigarettes and gasoline, it was an expensive day trip in terms of money, time, and dignity.

The girls ate, then once again disappeared into the playroom. I was a little surprised; I would have thought they would have spent more time with their mother. I expected to see each of them on their mother's lap, holding her, and being held, but there was very little of that. I wondered if things would be different if I were not there. Somehow, I didn't think so.

"It is amazing what goes on in this place. I live with about 50 women in a dorm. The food here is too gross to eat. The guards, even the men, watch you take a shower, it is such an awful feeling the way they look at us." Deb shared with me.

Throughout the time I was there, Mike and Deb held hands. The guard who didn't allow this type of behavior wasn't there. I looked around the room and watched as people sat and played cards or board games while doing a lot of eating and talking. It was much different than Attica where everyone was touching and kissing and children were exposed to things meant for behind closed doors. Directly next to us sat a black prisoner and her male friend. She was at least 350 pounds. She literally ate from the time she arrived until we were mandated to leave at 2:30 P.M.. She consumed at least eight bags of popcorn, two containers of chicken wings, and several candy bars! The poor man she was with must have spent a fortune at the vending machines, not to mention the exercise he got! I subsequently found out that she was in for drug charges.

A few moments later I noticed a guard come out with a woman. There were shackles around her feet and waist. I watched the guard remove the handcuffs and shackles and hang them in a closet. She was seated behind a barrier, away from the other prisoners and close to the guards. I later learned that prisoners have the right to see their visitors regardless of their behaviors in the prison.

Deb decided to go over to the children's room to be with the girls for a little while. She was one of the workers during the visiting sessions and had more freedom than many of the other prisoners. Deb returned alone.

"The girls wanted to play by themselves and watch a movie."

A little while later I walked back to the children's center. I was trying to give Mike and Deb some time to be alone. For some reason the guards didn't mind my going into the children's room. Inside, Catrina was watching a Disney movie.

"How are you doing?" I asked as I put my arm around her shoulder.

Catrina just shrugged—no answer, no emotion. She never turned away from the TV. Why wasn't she with her mother? Why didn't she show any emotion when her mother walked into the visiting room? It is so unfair to the children to expect them to sit at tables for six hours. Would it be so bad to have a place where they could curl up and have that closeness a child needs so badly with her mother? Beth was playing a game by herself on the carpet. I sat beside her to see how she was doing. She gave me a big smile but didn't say anything. I smiled back and rubbed her shoulders.

I returned to the visiting room. Deb started talking about the different women and why they were in there. Drugs were a major factor and more than a few of them had embezzled money from their employers. As I looked around the room I also noticed that the majority of women were black, but what surprised me more was that there were no black children visiting that day.

Catrina and Beth finally came back to the table. Catrina immersed herself in her coloring while Beth started playing cards. She had brought along a game and wanted to play, but neither of her parents were interested. They seemed mostly focused on conversing with me. Unfortunately, the conversation which was about to transpire was not for children's ears.

All of a sudden a guard yelled "roll call." The prisoners all got up and went to the center of the room, standing in a straight line while facing the guards. Once lined up, they shuffled to the open area where the vending machines and children's room were. I could hear the guards yelling out the prisoners' names and the prisoners acknowledging. Catrina would probably think this was part of college since we also have roll call during our fire drills at school. Fifteen minutes later, Deb returned to the table and rolled her eyes.

"I can't understand why they do this," Mike said angrily. Where do they think they are going to go?"

I couldn't help but wonder why, at the maximum security prison at Attica, there was no roll call, yet here there was.

"Well, one woman recently escaped from here," Deb explained. "She pretended to be asleep and the guards just counted her as being here until one finally realized that she was gone. So now, they make everyone stand and be counted when they are in their bunks. Why they do it here?" she asked rhetorically. "They were embarrassed that they lost a prisoner."

All the while, Catrina and Beth could hear and see everything that was going on. I silently hoped that they wouldn't grow up thinking college was like this! I was surprised to learn that Deb had a college degree. This was a woman who understands college. It wasn't fair for her to do this to her children.

Deb started sharing stories with me, and by the look on Mike's face I could tell that he had heard them all before. "There is a woman here who killed her husband and their dog. That wasn't the worst of it. She then cut the dog's head off, then cut her husband's head off, switched them, and then sewed them on each other. She then buried them together."

"Is this a good idea to be talking about this with the girls here?" I whispered.

"They're coloring and not paying attention to us." Deb dismissed my concern with a wave of her hand as though it wasn't a big deal.

It didn't seem to matter to Deb and Mike that the girls were listening to everything, yet it bothered me. They were still coloring and looking as though they were oblivious to the tales, but I knew better.

Women started leaving one by one. I noticed that, if their visitors had made such a purchase, they were allowed to take two cans of pop back to their cells with them. They reported to the same guards who we reported to when we entered the facility. The female prisoners then walked to the opposite end of the room where they passed through double doors. They were then made to sit in a chair that bore a frightening resemblance to an electric chair, before disappearing into yet another room. About ten minutes later the prisoner would return.

"Deb, can you tell me what is happening down there as they leave the visiting area," I asked.

"When it's time to leave you give the guards your two cans of pop. You have to sit in the chair and it detects if you have any metal objects. When the guards clear you, you enter a room where you are strip-searched. They make you take off all of your clothes, spread your legs and bend forward for a hand search."

Catrina and Beth were still drawing, still listening. The conversation then switched to Mike's concern that his wife was going to become a lesbian.

"No I'm not," She replied, rolling her eyes as though that were preposterous.

"This is really hard for me, you know," Mike blurted out. "I don't like being by myself." He looked to me for sympathy.

It was a conversation I really didn't want to hear and it was a conversation that the girls never should have heard.

It was getting toward the end of the visit and I could sense the tension between Mike and Deb. The room was so noisy, it was difficult to think straight. Deb started telling Mike things to do with the girls, how to do their hair and what to feed them. I could sense Mike's disgust and I was glad the visit was almost over. I desperately wanted some peace and quiet, and I admired the way the girls were such troopers and so well behaved, I was very proud of them.

"It is not easy, you know, when I have so much to do," Mike continued. "I don't have time to do everything by myself."

"Well you need to make time." Deb replied in a dictatorial tone. "What about Catrina's birthday party, what are you planning to do for her?" She asked.

"Your sister is going to take care of it at her house." He replied.

"My sister is not running our house and I don't want her to have the party there. You do it," Deb commanded.

"All right," Mike snapped back.

It was apparent that they had completely forgotten about the girls during their conversations. Finally, acknowledging her daughter, Deb reached over and gave Catrina a hug. "Catrina, you have a fun birthday," she said lovingly.

I wondered how Catrina felt about her party after hearing all the arguing between her parents. I was also very surprised by the comments Deb made regarding her sister's involvement in her children's lives. Her sister was such an integral part of the girls' lives and I learned even more about her when, in response to a writing and illustrating assignment, Catrina wrote:

> One day my aunt asked us if we wanted to go to Canada. I said yes and my sister did. And my aunt said on next Tuesday only we said ok. So next Tuesday we went to Canada. We got a motel with water slide and a hot tub. As soon as we got are room I put my bathing suit on and then went swimming.

I couldn't help reflect how happy all of us at the school were to know that the girls' aunt was exposing them to many interesting opportunities aside from the weekly trips they took with their father to "college."

"I'm going to bring a treat to school," Catrina said with a smile, looking at me for approval while at the same time bringing me out of my reverie.

"Well that's a good idea and your friends at school will like that too!" I told her.

Mike went to the vending machines to get the two milks Deb was allowed to take back to the "dorm."

"Did you color me a picture?" Deb asked Catrina.

"No, this is for Ms. Martone."

She never lifted her head from the paper when she answered her mother, she just kept drawing. It took all my strength not to cry. The whole time there I thought she was drawing a picture for her mother; instead, she drew a picture of herself and one of her sister in a park . . . for me!

"To Ms. Martoon from Catrina." I wondered if she knew in her heart that her mother was not allowed to take the pictures back to her "dorm" room to hang on the wall. I wondered if she knew that the guards made her throw them away.

All I could do was thank her and give her a big hug. "I'm going to hang this right on my refrigerator and I will think of you every time I see it!"

Little Beth came over to me and wanted a hug too. It was as though she thought I was going to remain behind with her mother.

"I'm in a hugging mood today!" I said as we gave each other a huge bear hug.

We walked to the exit area and for the last time, until next week anyway, there were more hugs and kisses for the girls and Mike. Deb shook my hand and thanked me. Back once more through the gates and buzzed in areas. It was so bitter cold out!

"I'm telling you, I love her and hate her at the same time," Mike said to no one in particular.

The drive home was quiet, and the girls fell asleep. Going to "college" to visit their mother was a long day.

Over the course of time, the situation between the children's parents has grown progressively worse. The tension has increased to the point of Mike wanting to file for a divorce. He shared with me that this way of life is too hard and he is tired of being harassed every week by his wife. I believe he is simply overwhelmed and tired of everything. The only problem with a divorce is that Catrina is not Mike's biological daughter and would remain with Deb's sister. Beth would no doubt go with her father, thus splitting up the girls at a critical time in their lives.

After I learned of this possible future for the children, I also learned that Mike had a mild heart attack—yet another devastating downturn to any stability that was possible in their lives. Fortunately, their aunt came to their rescue and took the girls into her home and into her arms of love. Catrina is now on an anti-depressant, and the transformation has been remarkable. She is happy, full of smiles, and acts very much like a "normal" child.

Through a class writing project, I learned that Catrina's birthday turned out to be a very special event:

> My aunt invited me to her house for my birthday sleep over. I was so exciting I new we would have fun. The next morning I packed my book bag up. I brang a pair of socks underwear toothbrush beany bears little beany, medium beany and also big beany. I went to my aunts and the girls were there the first thing we did was had a dance party. And then we eat dinner. And after that we went in the basement we played. And then my cousin called us up for a craft. And after that we put makeup on I had it all over my face. And then I took pictures and then we set up our sleeping bags and I fell right to sleep.

What a relief for us to read her writing and learn that her special day turned out to be perfect for a little girl whose aunt truly is her "fairy godmother." I admire this little girl, who is a pillar of strength for her father and sister. In the eyes of the school she is a heroine, a model for all little girls to look upon and admire. We have no doubt in our hearts that she is going to make it despite the turmoil.

No Ifs, Ands, or Buts about It

THE CEPHAS HOUSE IN Rochester, New York is a residential home for inmates who are transitioning from the prison system back to society. After release from incarceration, Cephas provides support to adult individuals. Cephas offers short-term transitional housing (from 90 days to six months) for parolees. The mission is to assist parolees in making a successful transition into the community by providing a safe and supportive place to live and an opportunity to develop and practice newly acquired life skills.

Men who have successfully participated in a Cephas Prison Visitation Support Group, as well as other qualified referrals from the Division of Parole, occupy the residences. All participants must demonstrate a desire to change and take the steps necessary to become productive members of society. Cephas provides continuing support and guidance, access to health and rehabilitation services, and assistance in seeking and maintaining employment. The overall purpose is to re-integrate ex-offenders back with their families and into society with the additional goals of reducing recidivism, strengthening families, and making the community safer.

It is in this home that this story came to fruition. When I called and shared with the director, Robert Miller, my reason for wanting to meet with him and the work I was doing with children with parents in prison, he graciously invited me to visit. The home was located in the inner city, in a neighborhood of old, rundown mansions that in their day must have been sites of opulence.

My arrival and tour of the house spurred a great deal of curiosity, and the residents soon began to casually enter the room in which Robert and I were sitting. None of the residents made any eye contact with me or any acknowledgement of me until Robert introduced them. As we moved to sit at the dining room table we were already immersed in a rich dialogue and debate surrounding the issues of the prison system.

As the discussion began to focus on the impact the prison system has had on the children of parents who are incarcerated, one by one the residents of the home meandered into the dining room and were invited to join us. During the course of the conversations with this group of men, I listened to each of them tell their story and describe the devastating impact their wrong choices had had upon their families and their relationships with their children. The deep regret for the poor decisions they had made during the course of their lives weighed heavily upon them.

Suddenly, out of the blue, a young man divulged in a nonchalant manner that he and his father used to write to each other from their prison cells. The other men sitting around the table just looked at him with an understanding eye. His announcement piqued my interest and we arranged a time to meet. I wanted to learn more about this young man who shared the prison life with his father.

David had greasy blonde hair, green eyes, and a wholesome build. He maintained an extremely outgoing personality. In the few minutes we talked, he appeared somewhat arrogant, but I attributed that to his youth and to the environment in which he lived. During the course of the interview, I saw a young man who was living in an adult world from which he desperately wanted to escape. He was a 22-year-old who, despite his tough exterior, would obviously love to have his father in his life. This is his story, his pain, and his desire for himself:

"When I was 16, I told a kid who was 15 how to rob a house and he did it. I told him, if I told him how he had to give me half of what he got, so I got 600 dollars. When he gave me the money I went out and got my license and then had a party for a whole weekend. A month later investigators came to my home; the kid had told them what I did and they arrested me and took me to jail." He shook his head as if acknowledging his own stupidity. "The cops had an indictment for me which is greater than a warrant. A warrant isn't true; indictment is true. I knew I was going to jail."

"I was always under the impression that you are innocent until proven guilty. Did the cops arrest you based on a man's word?" I asked.

In an excited tone he blurted out, "Exactly! That's all they need. If he writes a statement, you're going to jail. An involuntary statement, it doesn't matter, you're going to jail. *Just for a piece of paper.* So they took me to jail."

"You were 16 years old at the time . . . what did your parents do?"

"My mom refused to bail me out. She left me there for a week saying, 'you're gonna learn your lesson.' So I said, 'I don't want to talk to you.' She finally came and bailed me out for 500 dollars. She hired me a lawyer and we fought the case for a year. I finally told 'em, 'listen, I got a job, and I'm going to school.'"

"Where were you working?"

"I was working on a farm as a herdsman for four hours a night after school. Since I was doing well they said they would give me a chance and so they gave me probation. I did 250 hours of community service and I paid back the 600 dollars.

"I really did try and do good but I just couldn't seem to keep it up. I drove recklessly about six or seven times and I had some assaults and petty larcenies, and bar fights. So that's what happened, 13 misdemeanors and two felonies cause I got into the wrong crowd. I met this kid who wanted to go rob cars and I went with him to rob cars. I didn't touch nothing but he said I did it, so they gave me another felony. And I had the grand larceny for supposedly robbing this garage that I never robbed. It just added up. And with my name, they said, 'Oop, it's gotta be him, he did it.' So in 1999, it all added up and they said I was going to prison."

"What was the final straw that landed you in prison?"

"The final straw was violating probation, using drugs, smoking marijuana. I stole gas every night from a farm tanker. One of the milkers seen me and said, 'You don't work here no more.' He told his boss and the boss pressed charges. The police were looking for me for like two weeks, knocking on my apartment door, trying to get in, but I wouldn't open the door for them. Then, one night, they seen my truck at my buddy's house and they knocked on the door and my buddy's dad said, 'Ah, yeah, he's here.' I didn't let my friend's dad know that the police were looking for me. When they finally caught up to me they threw me up against the trailer and said, 'You're under arrest for a warrant for petty larceny.'

"When I got to jail they said, 'No bail' because I violated probation. The police took me to court the next morning. The judge told me, 'You got caught driving without a license in three towns, petty larceny in three towns, and you stole 40 gallons of gas every night.' The charges added up and I knew I was going to go to prison. My mom offered to hire me a lawyer again. I said, 'OK'.

"My attorney told me, 'Listen, you can get a one-to-three year sentence. But because you're a youthful offender at 16, they'll also let you go to Shock Camp.' They made it look real good; 'Shock Camp' is like boot camp. So I went to boot camp."

"And what happened at Shock Camp?"

"They first sent me to Wende Correctional Facility to get my reception; you're like basically segregated from everybody in jail because you're a newcomer to the prison system. Then you go to Elmira, which is the same thing. That took three weeks. Then I went to a place called Lakeview, which is the head of Shock. When I got there they evaluated me and said I wasn't a violent offender and that I could go to minimum Shock camp, so then they sent me down to Monterey. Yup, shackled at the feet, chained to the waist, shackled with another guy, riding in a bus that felt like a hayride. It's a boot camp for young men who are under 18. I did 184 days. You gotta go do your time. *No ifs, ands, or buts about it.*

"It was degrading. It was very vulgar. One mean ride. There was a kid sitting behind me, he smiled, and one of the drill instructors smacked him in the face. They say it's a 'hands-on program.' 'We can put our hands on you; we can do anything we want to you. You're sent here because you committed a crime. This is what you're going to do to repay your crime.'"

"What was it like?"

"You wear greens and you wear a number on your chest that says your name and the year you came into prison and what number inmate you are. It was like a bunker, like a military bunker. You had everything military and some of these drill instructors that became correctional officers had been in service. You had to live in bunkers and you had to go everywhere marching. If you screwed up and you didn't pass all your evaluations in school, your military bearing, cleanliness in your cube, and your work— if you failed—they kicked you out of the program. You then went to do your time, whatever your time was, whether it was three years, two years, a year. . . . That's the benefit with Shock: you do the 184 days successfully, you get out of prison—*no ifs, ands, or buts about it.*

"If you can't make it at Shock Camp and if you go to prison, you have to see the parole board. The parole board looks at your file and they say, 'Well, nope, you ain't going home—you gotta stay another two years.' So that's what eventually happened to me; I went back to prison after getting hit at the parole board."

"What do you mean by 'hit'?"

"A 'hit' at the board is when they hold you for a period of time they think is going to be beneficial to you to be successful in society. They look at your paper, they look at your file, which has got everything in it from day one to the present, and they say, 'Oh, we don't think you're ready, we think you're a menace to society.' Commissioners, two of 'em, they say, 'We don't think you're ready.' They don't know you from a hole in the ground. They know your paperwork, that's all they know. They give you a chance to say a word but your word is not going to mean anything because the decision's already made when you go in there, and they say, 'No, I don't think you're ready,' so they can give you a period of 12 months to two years and hold you for that long. They held me for an extra year.

"When I finally got out, I moved in with my mom and I got a job working construction work with my uncle's construction company. I was naïve to the parole system and even though I knew I was supposed to ask permission to drive I didn't ask him personally, I asked another parole officer. I starting driving and the parole officer was following me home, I didn't know it was him. I shifted my truck into fourth gear and that's all I seen of him. I outran him and got pulled over by a state trooper and violated parole because I was driving without the permission of a parole officer. The state trooper pulled me over and arrested me, *no ifs, ands, or buts about it,* 'You're under arrest for violation and you're going back to jail.'

"Yup, that's where I've done all my crime was in Livingston County, Geneseo, New York, right where I live. I went to the county jail where the police told me everything I did wrong on parole. I got technical violations that you got to obey. There are so many rules and if you don't obey one of them rules it's called a 'technical violation' and you're going back to jail. I was then put under house arrest.

"Then, one night, I stole a car. The keys were in it. I just went out, jumped in it with the mindset that I was going to go beat the person up that put me in jail in 2000. I was going to go beat him with a baseball bat. So I went out looking for him but I couldn't find him so I came back to the city with the stolen car. I parked the stolen car right out in front of the Volunteers of America shelter, went home, like nothing was happening. Next day, I was riding around the city with the stolen car. Didn't care. I already committed the crime. I'm already going to jail as soon as they catch me.

"Three days after I stole it. I'm driving it like it's mine, racing all over the city with it. Going to gas stations, filling it up and driving away without paying. Did that like 10 times. Well, somebody seen me at the store that I was at so I took off. On the way taking off, I'm driving and I see somebody following me so I said, 'Okay, it's either one of two things. It's either somebody that knows me and they want to talk or it's the police.'

"Sure enough, I quickly signal to the right to see who it was. Cops came from everywhere so I blacked out and the first thing I do is run. So I hit first gear, shifted it into third gear, and took off. I was in a high-speed chase with the cops. As time went on, more cops added into the chase. And I was being so egotistical and so cool about everything. I was counting the cops through my rear-view mirror driving down the road at 120 miles an hour. I counted 15 of 'em. The cops are chasing me and they're still coming down left roads and right roads and I'm seeing them come.

"They're trying to swarm me. They're trying to set up traps and roadblocks and I'm blowing through all that. I cut through traffic, and almost killed a couple of people and next thing you know a school bus appeared on the road. So I'm driving, I'm trying not to concentrate too much on the school bus, but concentrate on the driving. I went through some S curves, sharp bends in the road and the school bus, I guess. I don't remember what happened to it; all's I remember is seeing it. I guess it veered off the road and went into the ditch. So right there I just committed a felony, but with the laws that are out there every kid on that bus is a felony. So there was 13 felonies, one for every kid, plus the school bus driver, so that's 14 felonies plus the stolen car, that's another felony so that's 15 felonies, I've added up for you already without even knowing it. The driver identified me on a first name basis."

"Did any of the children or bus driver get hurt?"

"No. Come to find out, nobody got hurt, no damage was done to the bus but they're still charging me with endangering these kids."

"Well, you did."

"Exactly. I endangered the kids. The driver identified me. I didn't stop when I seen that bus. I just kept it going. I know what road I'm on because I know Livingston County. I know it. I know every road in the county because I've outran cops on every road in the county. Literally. So I knew a stop sign was coming. I knew it but I thought it was a little ways up but I forgot about the hill. There was a knoll before the stop sign. Now, I'm going 120–125 miles an hour on cruise control, so I can concentrate on counting the cops instead of worrying about the gas. I'm just going one speed. I don't hit the brakes. I don't do nothing. If I need to brake, I pull the emergency brake and that's immediate stop. But I came up over the knoll at 120 miles an hour and the car went airborne. Gravity took over and I went flying across the road—no control. I went across the road and I was headed right for a telephone pole; I spun 180 degrees in the air. I was going across the road spinning and I smashed into the ditch. I missed the telephone pole by a foot. The car started flipping over at least four times."

"What did they do when they finally caught up to you?"

"They had six investigators with guns drawn. One had it right up against my temple as he yelled at me to get out of the car. I'm like, 'Yo, is my face bleeding?' Cause the airbag hit me. At 120 miles an hour the airbag smashing you in the face feels like you got knocked out so I'm worried that I'm bleeding. I'm not worried what I did, I'm not worried about going to jail, and I'm not worried about nothing but my face bleeding right now. So the cop says, 'No, it's not bleeding, get your hands up.' I couldn't get out because of my seat belt. 'Unbuckle your seatbelt and get out.' He pulled me out of the car yelling, 'Get out!' and threw me in the ditch.

"This investigator is the investigator that put me in prison the first time *and* the second time so he knew me. He lived up the street from me. He called me by my first name; I called him by his first name. He's about 6 foot, 250 pounds. He threw me in the ditch and immediately put his knee in my back and handcuffed me. 'What were you thinking? Where did you get the car? Are you hurt?' I asked him if I was bleeding. I ended up with a one-inch scar on my elbow and my back hurt and my ribs hurt. They told me they were taking me to the hospital. I'm like, nah, 'I don't need to go, just take me to jail.' They called the ambulance anyway and strapped me on the gurney. One of the police officers asked me if I was drinking when I took the car. I wasn't, but I told them I was drinking when I took it to give 'em a reason for me taking the car because they would think that me doing all this chaos, if I did it without a substance, they would really think I was crazy. So I was like, 'All right, yeah.' At the hospital they X-rayed me, I got five broken ribs. I told the doctor, 'I'll feel it in the morning.'

"So they took me to the conference room at the sheriff's office. One of the officers asked me what happened. I said 'I don't know.' She's like, 'You're in big trouble, that's what they say.' I said, 'All right, well, let's go talk to a judge.' I didn't believe nobody. I'm like, I couldn't have done that much. I stole a car, I got the keys, it's a mess in here. I don't know what else happened so they bring me into court, explain all this other stuff to me, what happened. They bring me to the worst town in the world to get arraigned in.

"They brought me before a judge, they woke him up cause by the time everything was done, said and over with and they took me to the hospital and all this other stuff happened it was like 1:30 in the morning. The judge was disgusted, 'All right, you've been here before, you've gone to jail before—50,000 dollars cash bail.' I said, 'Oh, yeah!' He said, '100,000 dollar bond.' I know I'm not getting outta jail because as soon as parole finds out about this, they're violating me. I was on parole and I stole a car so that means I was committing crimes on parole.

"So next thing you know the parole officer sees me as soon as I get to the jail. I said, 'How did you get here so fast?' He said, 'I was in the high-speed chase with you.' I told him the doctor told me I was lucky to be alive so, I'm great! I'm lucky to be alive? I should be dead right now! I'm going to jail but it doesn't matter as long as I'm alive. They processed me and let me make my phone call.

"At that point in my life, I had a public defender. Because I burned so many bridges with my family they told me, 'No, we're not supporting you.' A nobody attorney? They're no good because they're cheap and they work for the county. They work with the judge so they're on the judge's side, not my side.

"I got lucky, though, because the public defender that I got was my family court lawyer, because of all the family court visits that happened with my mom and dad for 10 years. When I was 12 years old my mom forced me into making a decision: "Do you want to stay with your dad, or do you want to stay with me?' Now, Mom had the structure. Dad was very dysfunctional with his drinking, using cocaine, doing all this other stuff, so…of course, I'm a momma's boy, I'm going to stay on living with my mom. My lawyer helped me through the family court so when she became a public defender she knew my background; she kinda pulled a few strings. She got the sentence down to 16 months to four years."

"Did your mother come and visit you?"

"No, Mom….Mom was way out of the picture by that point."

"Why was she out of the picture?"

"Because I told her: 'I'm always gonna do what I wanna do. You don't have nothing to say about it, I don't care if you're my mom. I don't care. It doesn't matter to me. I'm doing what I wanna do. And you want to chose your boyfriend over me so, screw you, if that's how it's gonna be. You choose your boyfriends over me until they screw you over.' To this day I still don't talk to her.

"You know, my mom used to tell me that she knew I would make it. She's told me this on numerous occasions. I'm like, 'Oh thanks, mom. Thanks for giving me the confidence that you knew I'd make it through this jail term, even though you weren't there for me because *I'm* a strong one.' I had to be. I pretty much raised myself because I had no attention. I've had a part-time job since I was 14 years old so it's always been like that. It's always going to be like that."

"What does your mother do?"

"My mom is a pediatrician and her whole side of the family is educated. One of 'em's a sheriff, three of them are teachers, one takes care of mentally handicapped people as a teacher, and my grandmother is a retired librarian. They all got these nice white-picket lives."

"And what about your dad?"

"Well, my dad's side of the family is another side of the fence: It's all hillbillies, they're all drinkers, they're all partyers and they all beat each other up. 'Let's get drunk! Brotherly love!' There's eight boys and one girl and they're all mechanics. My mom and dad is like the 'bad guy, good girl' image. That's how my relationships are, too: the 'bad guy, good girl.' Good girls like the bad guys. Mom don't talk to me. Never. She tried to talk to me but I cut her off. I said, 'No, if you want to jump out of my life that easy, you're not gonna have it. *No ifs, ands, or buts about it*—even at Christmas.'

"So, that means I was going back to prison. So they sent me to Livingston Correctional where I did eight months. Then I got good behavior and they shipped me to a minimum security facility. I seen the parole board, and they said, 'You're a menace to society; you're not going home,' and they held me for another year.

"So, I went to a minimum security work camp. You go out with a work crew all day long. You go perform community service, basically, and you go to towns and do work. You pick up sides of the roads, pick up cigarette butts at parks, and you do a whole bunch of degrading stuff. It's very degrading because you're in inmate greens with a correctional officer with a gun. And you're riding around in this big green van and everybody's looking at you. They're looking at you like you was going to commit a crime. You got A-1 murderers out in their town. *Of course* they're going to watch you. It's very degrading. You go out there and you work for measly 15 cents an hour doing all types of stuff. You're cutting down state forests, you're working with the Department of Conservation. And we're doing all this other work for *15 cents* an hour. You don't use no power tools. You're doing everything by hand. We cut fields down with a sickle bars like the old days. We don't have no weed whackers and all this other stuff. I ended up getting a job in maintenance so I didn't have to go out on these degrading crews. I was in the compound and I worked on the dormitories, the kitchen, and handyman type jobs all around the facility. Way better.

"So I went to the parole board again, and this time they granted me parole. When they granted me parole, they asked me to submit an address, which I did. I submitted another address cause they kept denying them. So I submitted like eight addresses and they said, 'Ah, you can't go to none of 'em.' So I said, 'What y'all trying to say?' The parole board told me to be prepared to wait a long time for a bed to open up in a shelter. So I wrote the director here at Cephas and told him the problem. I'd been writing him for a year and I wasn't sure what I was going to do because my dad had just gotten out of prison in Arizona so I wanted to go live with him. I really didn't want to, but it was my last resort cause I'd burned everything else, and he had done time so he was the only one who understood where I was coming from.

"My dad did five years in Arizona for threatening to kill his boss's family. My father is a mechanic. He's a decent mechanic so that's where I got that from. I am a junior so we got the same names. Our initials are 'DMV' so that's where I get the driving from. He's a driver, too. By the age of 35, he crashed 28 cars—totaled them, split Cadillacs in half, hittin' trees, got DWIs. This is the craziness of it: He rolled the car five times, got shot out the windshield, laid in a ditch, and a judge was driving by and seen him in the ditch and rescued him! We went and got my uncle's tow truck, put it on the tow truck and came home. He told me, 'Go get in the car and learn how to drive a stick shift.' I learned how to drive at nine years old.

"My dad left us and went to live the bachelor life: drinking, snorting cocaine, partying. My parents were always fighting, always arguing, and there was always domestic violence, and drinking—both of them drink. They separated and he left. He went back to the country and my mom stayed in town. The deal was that we would see my dad every weekend. Well, that never happened because my dad would say, 'Wow, I'm going to lose my weekends. I can't party on the weekends because I gotta go get the kids.'

"So we'd get all pumped up and motivated to go see him on weekends and he wouldn't show up. Why he wouldn't show up? There was three reasons: He was hung over, he was in jail, or he just didn't want to come and get us. It was as simple as that. He just wanted to party. And that happened numerous times. The chaos with my mom and dad is still going on.

"To the day, I think it's 30,000 dollars he owes in child support—or so my mom says. The domestic violence is still occurring even though she has a new husband. My dad would still come over cursing her out. I guess one time in 1996 he smacked her or something. He's in jail for that now because he came back from the Arizona prison and went on a cocaine binge, robbed a farm supply dealer who sells tractors in his home town, and got arrested for burglary, so he's doing a year in the county jail in Allegany County right now.

"My dad always used to try to buy my love. He bought me four-wheelers, he bought me dirt bikes, he bought me cars. I was eight years old and he's buying me cars and I'm driving around, up to a judge's house, down the street, through the yard. It didn't matter. I was going all over fields. But that's how I was raised. That's how it goes. My dad would say, 'If you're going to be a man, you're going to be a man now. You're going to do what a man does straight up. You either grow up or you don't do what men do.'

"I was going to bars at six years old; I used to ride my four-wheeler to the bar, by myself. The bartender would say, 'Hey, little Davy, how ya doing?' 'Yeah, can I get a dozen wings?' They'd give me it. Everybody at the bar knew me; that's how it was. My dad took me to the bar so much they knew me. So I'm like, 'Dad, I want some chicken wings' and he'd say, 'go get 'em.' I'd ride two miles on my four wheeler to the bar. That was at six years old.

"My mom knew it so that was the last straw to say, 'Yo, listen, get your dad out of the picture.' But it's going to be hard to get me away from my dad—even though I'm a momma's boy, I still got love for my dad."

"How did you get reunited with your dad?"

"I found out about my dad through my little brother's girlfriend. I guess he wrote her, because my little brother don't write. He has no care in the world as to what's going on. So she was there for support. She said, 'Your dad's looking for you.' So, I went through the process of talking to counselors, because you gotta get permission cause you're both incarcerated. They now read your letter that you sent him to make sure it ain't no, 'I'm breaking out of jail so meet me here on this date' kind of thing. That was very degrading. You know what I mean? You can't say what you want to say—because if you reminisce about old times they're going to find out about stuff. Anyway, they approved it and we started writing each other. He fed me the wonderful speech of: 'Oh, I'm sorry I was ruining your life for the last 10 years and all this other.' I believed him then, cause I was manipulating him because I knew I'd burned all my bridges except for him. I ain't burned him yet. He burned me. So he owed me something, so we started writing each other.

"From Arizona prison to New York prison, we've been writing each other for six months, and I haven't lost contact with him yet. He got out in 2001. He did two years on parole in Arizona and decided to come back to New York. But I guess when he finished his two years down there, he was doing good. When he came back to New York, he got back into cocaine: The monkey's on his back. The great cocaine addiction, the great alcohol addiction. He was back doing what he was use to doing. At 46 years old he had had three heart attacks and he's still doing what he was doing. He didn't care. He's hard-headed just like me. Doesn't care. 'What's going to happen is going to happen.'"

"What's going on with you and your dad now?"

"Me and my dad now? My dad's in jail, he won't get out till April. When he gets out, who knows because we were writing each other, we were writing each other a lot in jail. But in jail it's different because you have nothing to do so you want companionship. But now that I've got a life and stuff, I told him straight up, 'Man, if I don't write you, don't get mad, I've got things to do. I'm busy'. He said, 'All right, you're right. I love you, and I wanna be with your mother.' So I don't know what's going to happen when he gets out, really. You know, I want to go stay with him because I know. . . ."

"Does your dad write a lot?"

"I just actually wrote him a letter last week on a Sunday. He writes every so often. He writes when I write but I don't write that often because I've got things to do. Every couple of weeks I write him but I don't believe in making a relationship—reforming a relationship—in jail.

"We were both in jail, but it was more of, 'All right, we knew what was going to go on.' We were just talking junk. We was going to live with each other. It wasn't serious. You can't build a relationship in jail. That's why I refrain from building a relationship with my mother right now. I know how it is for my mom to come in there and see me in jail. I know how degrading it is having to go through metal detectors and doing all this other crazy stuff. When I got out of jail and she heard I was out, I got out two weeks before Thanksgiving. She'd heard I was out, she's like, 'Ohhhhhh.' And I'm like, 'No, you were not there when I was in jail, when I really needed you. Get outta here, I'm not trying to talk to you right now. Maybe after the holidays we'll talk.' They want to play the game so I'm just living my life. I have a girlfriend, I go to school and group; that's all I need. They weren't there for the last three or four years. I know how to live my life without them. It's sad to me but. . . ."

"Where are you going to go after your time here at Cephas House is up?"

"Where am I going to go? That depends on a lot of things. My employment status, school and the parole thing. But I got a week off from school, so I'm gonna look for a job.

"I know I max out on parole on May 31, 2006. On that date, I might be able to drive if New York State, if Albany lets me. Right now, I walk everywhere. The bus is very degrading to me just because I've always drove myself all over the place. I hate riding with people. I'm a fast walker. I learned from Shock, you learn how to walk."

"What made you decide to go to school?"

"My girlfriend is the one that got me into school. She's the one that helps me out with everything and she's more to me than my grandmother is to me right now. I don't talk to no family. I don't talk to not a single one. Nothing."

"But at least you're still touching base with your dad?"

"I try. I try."

"What do you talk about?"

"There, that's the bad thing. What do you talk about? When you're going to get out? What's going to happen when you get out? It's a whole lot of baloney, really. It's a whole lot of beating each other in the head. Actions have to speak louder than words, really. You can be all about the talking cause I can talk a good one but you gotta, you gotta prove it. My parole officer just came over the other night. He's like, 'Your old parole officer is asking about you.' I said 'Who?' Like the head boss down in the parole is asking about me. They got jokes all down there. 'How long is he gonna last until he goes back to jail?!' They got a little gambling pool— 'I bet he goes back to jail within six months, within a year.' Oh, yeah, they do a lot of that. But he is asking about me and they actually complimented me. He was like, 'You're doing good. Keep it up.' So I'm like, that's it. As long as I can do this—parole, get off parole. I do want to go stay with my dad but I don't. I wanna do what I gotta do."

"Are you going to try to get your dad to come to Cephas House or another transitional program?"

"Hell, no. He can't come to the city because he got that addiction. He knows too much of the city. In my belief, if you got addiction like crack, you're always going to have that addiction of crack. So you've got to keep 'em away from the 'great crack.' They be clean for all sorts of time and then all of a sudden, boo! Crack. I've never seen the stuff. I've only smoked weed and only drank. I never seen no other drugs and I've been in some bad neighborhoods and I still never seen 'em. My dad will tell you straight up, 'I can't go to Rochester. There's too much up there, it too tempting.'

"So, I think he's gonna stay in the country, which is going to be a problem. But if he gets on his feet I'm more than glad. But I don't know, I don't wanna live on my own. I gotta pay for this car; I owe 20,000 dollars for this car that's sitting in the junkyard right now that I crashed. I still have to pay for this thing and times are tough. I would love to live with somebody. Love it, but if it happens, it happens. Whatever is gonna happen is gonna happen in due time. With my girlfriend by my side, she's telling me I have to get back to my family when I'm ready. When that happens, who knows?

"I get asked how my career in the prison system is going. I've retired! It's not going to be my career. How much time did you do in your career? I say, 'my career?' It was five years. What did I lose? I lost a lot of respect, a lot of loyalty to my family. I lost of lot materialistic things. All this other stuff, and she calls it a career. So I call it a career, and I retired. And I retired at 20 years old. When they said you're lucky to be alive, I said, 'Oh yeah, I beat death once but we're not having it again. Nope. We can't do it no more.'"

"Do you think you're going to be all right or do you think you will end up like your dad?"

"Oh, I know I'm gonna be all right. *No ifs, ands, or buts about it.* Jail scares me. I break down and cry when I think I'm going back to jail. I seriously do.

"I thought I was gonna have a fight with one of these residents in here. Like the loose canon in here. I thought I was really going to rip his throat out, cut his throat out and feed it to him. And I was so devastated, I freaked out. I sat in the office and cried for like half an hour. I'm not going back to jail. No. No. No. I'm not going back to jail. I tell my girlfriend when we're driving, if I see somebody following us I'm like, 'Yo, let this schmuck pass us because I'm so afraid of the cops.' I let 'em all know me *ain't* going back to jail. No, there is no jail time in my future. *No ifs, ands, or buts about it.*

"I don't want to end up like my dad 'cause he started at my age. Like I told you when we talked before, at 15, he used to get kicked off the school bus or something, he used to hitchhike a ride with the milkman. So he started at my age and 30 years later, he's still doing the same thing. It's ridiculous. No, I'm done. It's over with. In 2006, I'm not a ward of the state no more. They ain't never going to see my name no more. No way!"

"So you're starting out with a degree in Human Resources. What do you plan to do with that degree?"

"Overall, it's going to mean counseling troubled adolescents and juveniles in the street. Juvenile delinquents, 'cause I feel that if I could do it to the hardest-headed kid in the world, in my book, which is my little brother, and I can get him to listen when he came to visit me . . . I smacked him straight in the mouth with my words, not physically, because I don't hit him.

"Most of these kids are in trouble because of school. They're not in trouble because they're committing the great criminal act. They're getting in trouble cause they don't wanna go to school. When you ask them, 'What ya here for?' they say, 'Cause I got put on probation because I didn't wanna go to school.' 'You didn't wanna go to school? Buddy, listen. I did five years. I wish I could of graduated school and walked down the aisle.' 'Are you kidding me! I don't wanna walk down no aisle,' they'll say. And I'll tell 'em, 'I got my diploma a year later cause I didn't have enough credits to even walk. It *killed* me. It *killed* me.'

"If I can get inside a kid's head, I *was* one. I just got it, ya know what I mean, I just got it. Everybody that's around me, that lives with me or that spent more than five hours with me will tell you, 'Oh, this kid's a leader.' It don't matter. I'm a leader. Get it? I was running a farm. I was 16. I was running a 2,000-cow farm by myself. Had people 50 years old under me, I was the boss of them at 16. I don't know, that's how I am. I'm a leader. It's very uncommon for me to say that I'm a leader and take compliments, but I'm just saying I am. That's what I wanna do with my degree. Something with kids, something to try and turn 'em around, cause kids is killing kids. *All the kids want is someone to be real for 'em.* They don't have dads that were there, or their dads were delinquent or dysfunctional, whatever you wanna call it these days. Somebody closer to their age can be that person. Ain't no better person than me in my book. That's how I feel. If I can't do it, nobody's gonna be able to do it. *No ifs, ands, or buts about it.*"

Sins of the Father

CYNTHIA, WE HAD A SITUATION on the bus," Kathryn, my secretary, announced right before my first sip of coffee. Kathryn is incredible at what she does. She essentially helps me run the school. In fact, the word "secretary" doesn't even begin to describe her. "Partner" and especially "friend" would be more like it. When she tells me we have a situation, I drop everything.

"What's going on?" I asked.

"Lakisha came in off the bus crying to her teacher that Robert Ryner told her he was going to get a gun and shoot her in the head."

"Where do these children learn these things? The cruelty among children just drives me nuts. Where do they learn to be so mean, so young?"

"She's out here; do you want me to send her in?"

"Yes, and thanks, Kathryn."

Lakisha came into my office—a beautiful little black girl dressed in a pink shirt with blue jeans and sneakers that flashed when she walked. Her hair was neatly pulled into a ponytail and tears filled her eyes.

"Lakisha, it doesn't sound like you're having a good day so far; can you tell me what happened on the bus this morning?"

"Robert told me he was going to put a gun to my head and kill me," she said through muffled sounds of crying and tears streaming down her cheeks.

"Lakisha, why do you think Robert said that to you?" I asked, kneeling down to be at eye level with her.

"I don't know," she said in a mumbled voice mixed with sobs.

Well, here we go again, I thought to myself, move over J. Edgar Hoover! This is not the type of thing little girls in kindergarten make up. The increase in the number of children killing these days brings the word "investigation" to a new level. Reports are taken, police and parents are called, and everything is documented for tracking the child to see if tendencies for the unthinkable are even remotely possible.

"Kathryn, could you get Robert Ryner and have him brought to my office?" I yelled out.

"Right away," she yelled back.

So much for using the intercom, a daily joke in the office since I never use it.

"Ms. Martone, here is Robert," Kathryn announced a few minutes later as she walked him into my office.

Robert was a second-grader with neatly cut brown hair, brown eyes, and tidy clothing—a nice-looking young man. It was the first time he had been to my office. He wasn't a child who stood out on any of my classroom visits. He never came up to hug me, or show me his work, or ask me a question. I never would have predicted in a million years the things this child was capable of. I wish I had enough time to get to know all of my students on a personal level.

"Robert, have a seat." I motioned him to the chair.

"Did you tell Lakisha that you were going to take a gun and shoot her in the head?"

"Yes," he replied sheepishly, his head down.

"Why would you say such a mean thing to her?"

He shrugged his shoulders, but said nothing.

"Robert, why did you threaten Lakisha? Did she say or do something to you that made you angry?"

Looking at the ground, he shook his head "no."

I was to learn later through a conversation with the teacher that his father told him black people were bad, and Robert picked on Lakisha because she was black.

It's standard to document everything—especially when a weapon is mentioned. I'm always concerned with the possibility of access to weapons in students' homes. I called the police, and after a failed attempt to reach Robert's mother, I called his grandmother. Robert and I waited in the office together. I didn't say anything, I just watched him. I was amazed that he made no attempt to talk, he just sat there. It wasn't normal for a child of his age to be so quiet. Generally, when children come into my office for a discipline problem I talk with them; they always end up talking to me as though nothing happened. They talk about their dogs or mention something about the Asian water fountain on my desk. Not this child. Not a sound, not even a tear.

The police officer arrived first. I met him in the front office.

"We have a student who threatened to kill another child by shooting her in the head. I'm concerned about guns in the home and the threat. I'm sorry to have to bother you but I felt this needed attention and formal documentation."

"No problem," he replied.

We walked back to my office; Robert was still sitting at the table with his head down.

"Officer, this is Robert."

I motioned to the officer to sit. He tried but was unable to fit into my office chair. He was a large man, and ended up just standing and leaning against the wall. You could tell he was a little embarrassed. He didn't look like your typical police officer. In addition to being very large, he must have had lazy eye in both eyes. Making eye contact with him was difficult so I tried to avoid looking at him. Instead, I focused on Robert.

"Young man, your principal tells me that you threatened to shoot a little girl in the head. Is that true?" His voice was stern.

"Yes," Robert whispered, head still down.

The officer opened his report pad and began asking Robert a series of questions, his voice still serious. "What is your name?" "Where do you live?" "Who do you live with?" "Are there any weapons at the house?" Robert answered each question in a soft and respectful voice.

The phone rang. It was Kathryn informing me the grandmother had arrived. "Could you call Robert's teacher, Mr. Peller, and have him come to my office and get someone to cover his class? Excuse me, Officer, the grandmother is here." I went to the outer office to meet her.

Robert's grandmother looked like she'd had a very hard life. She was dressed in a sweatshirt and jogging pants with dirty sneakers that were once white. Her hair was a mixture of gray and blond, a little past her shoulders and disheveled as though she had just come out of a windstorm.

"Hello, I'm Ms. Martone, the principal. I have some upsetting news that I need to tell you before we go into my office," I began. "Mrs. Heitz, Robert threatened a little girl and told her he was going to shoot her in the head with a gun."

"I knew something like this was going to happen one day," she blurted out in a disgusted voice.

"Under the circumstances, I had to call the police and make a report. The policeman is in my office with Robert right now," I said as we walked into the room. I introduced the grandmother to the police officer.

"Hello," she said in a very upset voice, as though the officer were the problem.

"What did you do!" she yelled at Robert as she went over to him and hit him in the back of the head.

The policeman immediately announced in his firm voice, "We don't need any of this display." The grandmother backed off, looking at Robert with blazing eyes.

There was a knock at the door. It was Mr. Peller, Robert's teacher. At six-foot-four—and built like GI Joe, with a military haircut to boot—he towers over the second-grade children, but he has the disposition of a saint. He's always calm, and the children just love him. I made introductions again.

The police officer asked Mr. Peller if Robert had ever done anything like this before. "No, Robert is a good student, does all of his work and gets along well with the other students. If you ask him to do anything he'll do it right away. This is a big surprise to hear this news." His voice could not contain the disbelief he was feeling.

All of a sudden the grandmother started yelling at the child, "Why don't you tell them what you do to your mother?! He throws big rocks at his mother when she's doing the dishes," showing us with her hand the size of the rocks. "He's going to kill her one day if one of those rocks should hit her in the head." Her voice was almost to the point of screaming. "Did you tell them how you don't listen and how you threaten your mother with knives, that you're going to cut her up?!"

She got even more agitated, her voice rising in tone and anger. "He won't listen to his mother; he is mean to her!" Looking at the child and shaking her finger at him, she shouted, "Did you tell them how you swear at her with filthy language, how you say, 'Fuck You,' and call her a bitch? He even draws pictures of her bleeding, with him holding knives in his hands. Go on, go on, and tell them all the mean things you do to your mother." You could see the veins protruding from her neck.

Turning to us she uttered, "My daughter lives in fear." Her pleading voice was crackling as though she were about to cry.

"You're a bad boy!" she yelled at him. "You're just like your father. His father is mean and would hit my daughter," she snapped. "He's just like him—evil. Do you want to end up in jail just like your father?"

"No," he mumbled while shaking his head at her.

"Go ahead, tell the police how you held a hammer over your mother's head and told her you were going to kill her if she didn't get out of bed—she was so sick."

She looked at us in such a despairing way as though telling the "sins" would somehow relieve the pain she was in. "Go ahead, tell them how you told your mother that she had to go to sleep *sometime*." He doesn't do that for me because he knows I won't take it. He is also seeing a psychologist—Dr. Halt. I'm going to tell her what you said to that little girl."

We couldn't believe what we were hearing. I could see the anger growing in the officer as he listened to the shocking revelations. It was not hard to see that this was a new experience for him. Mr. Peller and I just looked at each other in disbelief. Neither of us had ever heard of anything like this before. In a million years we would never have dreamed that this child could be such an angel in school and so emotionally distressed at home.

The officer could no longer contain himself, "Young man, I never want to hear you do such a mean thing again. Do you understand me?" His voice filled with anger and disgust at what he had just learned. "Young man, if I find out you hurt your mother anymore I will come to the house and arrest you myself. Do you understand me?"

Robert nodded. "Yes." There were still no tears.

Once again, the grandmother could not contain her fury. "You're going to be in jail just like your father by the time you're 12!"

It was time to calm everyone down; the dirty secret was out. "Robert, I think you have been through a lot today and I believe you need some help to deal with all the anger you're feeling. For now, I want you to go home with your grandmother," I said.

The grandmother spun around, her face filled with fear. "Please don't let him stay at home, he may hurt her," she pleaded.

"Would you please tell your daughter that I would like her to bring him to school in the morning? I will give him in-school suspension until we can see what our next step will be, and it would be better than leaving him home during the day."

"Thank you!" She motioned to Robert to follow her and they walked out the door.

The police officer, Mr. Peller, and I just looked at each other with the same expression of disbelief. "There is no way I could allow that child to stay at home with his mother under these circumstances. I'm afraid of what he might do to her in a fit of anger now that he knows we are aware of everything." They both agreed.

"Thanks, Mr. Peller, for all your help, and my thanks to you, Officer. I appreciate the support." I sat in my chair, physically and mentally drained. I could not believe all that I just heard. I also couldn't believe that this child never shed a tear the entire time. It just wasn't normal; there was no sense of regret. More importantly, there was no fear whatsoever, not even of the police. I contacted the school counselor and psychologist. I needed help to deal with this, and the child needed help as well.

That night, I couldn't sleep. Images kept coming to my mind about the hammer and Robert cutting his mother with knives. Dear God, he was only in second grade! I remember reading about a little boy who was ridden with anxiety, and began to mutilate himself. He pulled out his permanent teeth. Why was I thinking of all these things! I was so tired; I just wanted to sleep.

The following day, Robert arrived at school with his mother. She was a pretty woman who barely reached four-foot-eleven. From the moment I met her I knew she was sweet and caring. As we spoke, I could see she had a simple mind. It was no wonder the child intimidated her the way he did.

"Good morning! I'm Ms. Martone, the principal," I said, extending my hand to shake hers.

"Hi, I'm Robert's mom, Nancy Ryner," she responded in a gentle voice. Robert was standing next to her. Head down, he said nothing.

"Robert, I would like you to sit here in the outer office while I talk with your mother.

"Why don't we go into my office, where we can talk?" I motioned her to the door. Once in the office we sat at the table. "Mrs. Ryner, your mother shared with us a lot of information about things that are happening to you. It is my intent to try and get Robert and you some help."

"Oh! Thank you! I really need some help with Robert. I'm afraid of him," she said, her childish voice full of fear.

"Can you tell me a little history of what's happening and what's going on with you and Robert? Your mother made some pretty scary accusations yesterday."

"Robert told me that his dad called and told him to put a pillow over my head and kill me when I'm sleeping. Robert calls me 'stupid,' 'dumb,' 'worthless,' and he hits me, just like his dad. He yells at me to 'pick up this filthy house.' I was so depressed, one time I couldn't look in the mirror and I was losing weight. He knows his father is in jail, but I try to brush it off. And I'll just say that Daddy is bad and he has to stay in there for a little while, but he will come back out. I fear that he may one day take Robert from me just to get back at me."

I questioned her about some of the things Robert was doing to her, for my own understanding and to see if there was any truth. It was so hard to believe, I was hoping that the story got blown out of proportion by her mother. I was in no way prepared for what she was about to tell me. I had a million questions to ask her but the one I was most concerned about popped into my head.

"When did your husband tell Robert to put a pillow over your head while you were sleeping?"

"I don't remember; he had called Robert from the jail."

"Did he attempt to do it?" I asked, startled.

She hesitated, then said in a low voice, "No, no, he didn't. He didn't."

The way she told me, I wondered if he had and she was afraid to tell me. "My God!" was all I could say. I just could not believe what I was hearing. As principal, I'm supposed to project a sense of authority, as though this was all in a day's work. But this situation was completely outside my frame of reference.

My thoughts were interrupted when she laughingly said, "The kid needs to be in *The Enquirer*, pretty soon he's going to be on *20/20*."

"What is Robert's father's name? "

"James—Jimmy—James," she responded hesitatingly.

"What do Robert and his father do when they're together?"

"That, I don't know because I'm not with them. He's not supposed to be around me because I have an order of protection. So, I don't want to be around him because it's like, as soon as I get around him, you know, the flowers come, then I'm roped back in. So I'm not even like that any more; I just don't want to be with him. I don't stay with him, my mom drops him off for like, three hours, and then she picks him up. I don't know what they do."

"What did you do when you were together as a family?"

Her thoughts were scattered and fragmented. She spoke so incoherently; it was difficult to follow what she was telling me.

"Um, nothing, really. I mean he bought the kid everything he wanted, not everything Robert wanted, but everything James wanted, like, if James wanted a scooter, he'd get it for Robert." She was leaning into me and whispering as though he were around to hear it. "He would rather do his drugs. He was always high. I was really, really embarrassed several times.

"Robert and I would do things alone. My mother kept saying, 'Nancy, when are you going to stop bringing him if he doesn't want to go?' I would bring Jimmy because I thought it would be a help. He would be a help, he was *no* help, and I had to help him *and* Robert. I really had my hands full because he was always on medication."

"What does he take medication for?"

"Um, for manic depression. He would get really, really high then really, really low. And it was a constant battle with him. I always had to make sure—'Jimmy, you taking your medication?' Besides Jimmy, I mean besides taking care of Robert too." She took a deep breath as though reliving the moment.

"Does Robert take any medicine, or did the doctor ever say that he may have these tendencies?"

"I thought I seen that in him one time because the kid would come out of school crying all the time." I could hear the pain in her cracking voice.

"One time he bit somebody in the leg right through the pants and made him bleed. It turned out to be my aunt's neighbor. She was mad!" Her voice raised with excitement.

"Well, I would be angry too, if my child were bitten," I interjected.

"I know. Not only that, it's embarrassing. You know I'm going to get sued one of these days and I don't have anything to offer them. What do I have to offer, my coffee filter?" She laughed. "I mean, I don't have anything to offer them. I'm trying to do well for me and Robert. I talk to him as a grown-up, 'Robert, you have to,' because he is really smart. 'You know I am trying to do good for us honey, so I can buy the toys you want and I can do better for you, and I can send you where you want to go, like, activities that are going on.'"

"Your mother mentioned a psychologist that Robert is seeing. What has Dr. Halt been doing? Does she talk only to Robert or to both of you together?"

"For like, the last 10 minutes she says, 'Mom, can you leave the room for a little while?' 'Yeah. Okay.' And I believe they put, like, he draws pictures. I've asked him to draw pictures of me and then I talk to him about them. I'm learning from them."

Leaning in toward me, she whispered, "And he's drawn a picture of himself holding a steak knife and the mother was bleeding—I was bleeding!"

"Oh my God!" I was sick at what I was hearing. Throughout the conversation I could see that she began to trust me and seemed grateful that I was taking an interest in her and, even more so, that I was taking a personal interest in her son.

"Did your husband ever use steak knives on you?"

"Oh, no," she blurted out in a gasp, as though I asked a stupid question.

"What did he do?"

"I called the police one time 'cause I got to do it ever so secretly. You know. He came after me and he sprained my arm and twisted it in the back of my head. That's the first time. He freaked out, you know, that's when he hurt me."

"Did Robert see any of this?"

"Um, Robert did, yeah," she whispered to me. "I mean, I always tell him if you're going to hit me, don't do it in front of the kid. I mean, I don't want him to do it anyways. When I say, 'No, Jimmy, we are not doing that,' or when I say 'I don't want to go here,' I would end up doing things I don't want to do."

"Does Jimmy call you from the jail?"

"He's called my mother a couple of times. You know what he says? I'll make you laugh about it. He's wrote me, like notes and letters and goes, 'You don't have a chance, Nancy, of getting Robert.' 'Okay, Jimmy, who's in jail?' I'd tell him. He's done time since he's been young but I'm not sure for what. I mean, what is he going to do, *bring the kid to jail with him?*

"Before I married him I seen the violence, I was so foolish, you know. Well I'm 23 and I wanted to get married, you know. 'Cause like nobody wants to marry me. My mother said, 'You married the wrong one.' I did, I snuck out, I did," she admitted as she laughed at herself. "Because I never told her I got married; I just went and got married. The way I got married she was mad, because I got married in pedal pushers and a tank top." She started laughing. "And just some strangers off the street signed the paper and the next thing I know I was saying, 'I do.' It just seemed like after I got married, it just seemed like it got worse, we fought more than we got along. He used to push me down and the—um, where we used to live in the trailer park, we could have sold tickets," she continued, laughing hysterically.

It was all I could do to hold back the tears. Nancy was laughing, but I didn't think it was funny. Part of me wanted to shake her and the other part wanted to hold her and make it all go away. I was concerned about her impaired parenting abilities and the father's too, and I was trying very hard not to be judgmental, but I was so angry. I didn't think they realized the devastating impact this lifestyle was having on their son.

"What jail is he in?" I asked.

"He's in the county jail till June 15th."

"Do you let Robert go to the jail to visit his dad?"

"No, you don't think that's a good idea, do you?" She asked as though she were looking to me for the right answer. "You know it bugs me when I hear others say, 'let's get all ready to go and visit Daddy in prison.' I don't think it's a good idea."

"I don't have the right answers for this," I confessed. "I do know that there are children who visit their fathers in Attica."

I couldn't help comparing what Robert would see and feel if he visited his father in the county jail, versus what the children who visited their fathers in Attica Prison saw. Although Robert wouldn't be exposed to the repugnancies the other children had to witness while visiting their fathers, he would have to be "wanded" before entering the sterile visiting room, with its light paneled walls, brown tweed carpeting, and faux bamboo seats that look like hourglasses.

Once inside, Robert would sit at one of the three U-shaped, counter-style tables, like the kind in a New Jersey diner. There would be no vending machines where he could get himself something to eat. Signs on the wall would demand, "Children Must Remain on Your Lap or Sitting in the Chair Not the Tables," or "Hands Must Remain on Tables."

The visits here would not allow Robert to touch his father's face nor play with his hair, and he would never be able to run and jump into his father's lap. Heaven forbid if a child needed to use the bathroom, because a sign clearly stating, "Once You Exit the Visiting Room You Cannot Re-Enter Including Bathrooms" forbade it. Also, there would never be three-day weekend visits— only two one-hour visits per week.

"When did he go into jail, and for what reason?"

"He assaulted me in October and pushed me down. I wish Robert would have never seen that," she said, while leaning toward me and whispering, "It's like the kid can't get it out of his head. You know, I have a phone and the courts gave it to me to call 911.

"Jimmy would come home daily and tell me, 'I'll cut your face with a razor the next time you're in the bathtub' or 'I'll slice your throat.' When he was 17 he punched the teacher."

The events and things that have happened to her were all over the place. So I just let her talk while I listened. I wondered if I should contact the husband and talk to him, but I was afraid he might go after her.

"In April he hit a police officer and then was arrested again. One time he showed up at three o'clock in the morning at my house. I opened the door and he was full of blood. Somebody had hit him in the face with a brick. His face looked like the hunchback. I just couldn't stand it anymore." Her voice trailed off. "I will never get married again."

"Me either." We both laughed.

"I'm trying to be a good mom, but he will be shaking hands with his father in jail. But I hope not, because I don't want him going down that road. Robert is just like his father, he'll yell at me, 'I'll strangle you, hit you and punch you until you can't breathe.' I mean, I love my kid with all my heart, but I didn't know being a mom was this hard. I don't know what I can do to help him."

A quick glance at the clock interrupted our discussion. "Oh, my! I didn't realize how late it was getting to be. Well, I better let you go. We will talk again."

"Do you ever bring Robert in here to talk to you?" She continued on.

"Yes, I had him in here yesterday."

"Do you think you could have him draw pictures for you?" she pleaded. "That way we can send them to Dr. Halt."

"That's a very good idea, I'll do that. Thank you for everything, I'll talk to Robert and keep you informed."

We had been talking for two-and-a-half hours! I couldn't believe we spent that much time together. I don't know how psychologists do this. I was mentally drained from all that I had learned. I'm supposed to be a pillar of authority, but the things I was hearing made me feel so naïve. I wish I could think of the poet who once said, "Times like these try men's souls." He was so right. My thoughts were rambling, I was tired, and I had five more hours to go.

The next morning I called Robert into my office. "Good morning! Have a seat at the table. I thought it might be a good idea if you and I chatted a little bit about everything that is happening and what you are feeling."

"What do you mean by, 'What do you think I'm feeling?'" he said in a sheepish voice.

"Robert, the police are now involved in your life and you do some pretty mean things to your mother. What are you thinking about all this stuff? That's what I mean."

"I think I'm feeling really, really bad," he said in a low voice.

He never looked me in the eyes when he talked. I wish I knew what he was really feeling. There were just no signs of remorse, or for that matter, any emotion at all.

"Robert, have you talked to your dad lately?"

"When he was just about to move, but I have no clue where he is moving," he shrugged.

He answered in a way that I didn't believe him. I think he was trying to protect his father. This unconditional love that children feel for their parents . . . it just baffles me sometimes.

"Have you talked to Dr. Halt about what you do to your mother?"

"Yes," he replied, his head hung down.

"What does she say to you?"

"She tells me to try and stop doing that, and I'm trying to stop doing it. I get really angry." His voice was so low and whining, I could hardly hear him.

"Robert, this is very upsetting for everyone but I'm going to tell you that I'm going to be checking on you and your mother often. I really don't want to hear, ever again, that you are doing those mean things to your mother. Do you understand me?"

"Yeah."

"Tell me, what do you like to do? Do you play any sports or have any games you like to do?" We chatted some more and I learned that he liked to play the violin. I was surprised to hear he was taking lessons.

"Do you think you can bring your violin into school and play me a song tomorrow?"

"Sure," he said with a look of surprise on his face. It was the first time there was any reaction to anything from him.

"I have an idea! Your mother tells me that you like to draw. How about drawing me a picture?" I gave him some paper and crayons. I was hoping that in conversation with him I could learn what he was feeling.

"While you're doing that I'm going to do a few things at my desk." As I watched him I could not believe that this child was capable of the cruelty that he could do to his mother. He worked so intently on the picture, with careful attention to every detail. He didn't talk the whole hour he was in my office. The silence was eerie. I so wanted to know what he was thinking and feeling after all that had happened to him. Was he glad it had come out in the open? I also wondered if he knew exactly what he was doing. This child was smart, street smart. Was he trying to manipulate me? God, I hate being made a fool of.

"What are you drawing?"

"It's a picture of me playing soccer. I like to play soccer." Looking up at me he then quickly put his head down and continued to draw. Still no smile and no emotion.

I just sat there watching him. I believe he was screaming for parameters to be placed on him. Screaming for help, but until then no one was listening. Well, he got our attention. Dear God, what next?

It was May and school would soon be out. His dad would be out of jail June 15th. His mother had decided to move to an apartment in a different school district. In the fall, Robert would be going to third grade in another school, in another district, with another principal. I was not about to let him slip through the cracks. While he was here, I checked on him frequently and called his mom to see how things were going at home. I called Robert into my office several times in addition to checking with Mr. Peller regularly. Both mother and son seemed to be doing better. But Robert also knew we were monitoring his behavior at home with his mother. I wondered how long this would last when he realized no one was monitoring him.

The end of the school year came quickly with the usual hustle and bustle of shutting down one year and beginning to look at the next. I was pleased that Robert went through the remainder of the school year without an incident. It wasn't until shortly after the following school year began that we received a phone call, requesting information from Robert's teacher.

I decided to call Robert's mother and see how things were going. "Nancy, this is Ms. Martone, Robert's principal from last year. I'm calling to find out how things are going with Robert and you and how he's doing at school."

"Things aren't going so well. He's angry all the time. He breaks pencils when he's doing his homework. I tell him to do something and he says, 'Fuck no!' to me." Her voice was desperate. "He doesn't listen at school; he's seeing the school counselor. This morning he didn't want to get up, or wash his face. I go through this every morning. It's almost like dealing with an autistic child or something. I don't know, he just likes to play games in the morning or something like that. 'No, Robert, we're not doing that right now.' I took his Game Boy away from him and he got mad. I'm trying to keep really cool but he gets me so nervous when he starts getting defiant and throwing things. 'Nope! Nope! I'm not going to do it,' he yells at me."

She continued on, "You know what's really sad? I'm going to come out and tell you. When I don't hear from Jimmy in three months or so, my mother and I just look at each other and we shake our heads and laugh! I bet you a dollar and a dime that he's in jail. Sure enough, and we get a phone call, you gotta laugh! This is an inmate James Ryner, calling collect, will you receive the call?" She laughed at the thought.

"And at one time I was, and I didn't know it was costing me like, six bucks. My mother put a block on my phone. He's been arrested so many times. One time he got arrested for stealing a color TV from Wal-Mart. Another time he broke the order of protection and he got six months for that. I'd tell him, 'Jimmy, you know you are not supposed to be here.' 'Yeah, Yeah,' he tells me and did it anyway."

"But of course, I have a baby with Jimmy and then there's a bond right there. You know, I mean I love Robert, I would never do," her voice trailed off. "When you get married and you have a kid it's different. When you don't have any kids you can just, just walk away."

"Is Robert seeing his dad at all?"

"He only takes Robert every other weekend and that really hurts him cause he loves his dad. But he is busy with his girlfriend, and at least he leaves me alone."

After speaking with her for an hour and a half, I could hear her doorbell ring over the phone.

"Nancy, I'll give you a call next week and we can talk some more," I said, trying to politely withdraw from the conversation.

"Oh, okay, I guess. You will call me next week?" There was urgency in her voice, as though she thought she would never hear from me again. "I can always come and visit you at the school if you would like some time?"

"Yes, I'll give you a call next week and if you would like to come and visit me at the school I'll buy you lunch. Talk to you soon."

I called the school where Robert was and left a message for his teacher to call me. Two days later the call came through.

"Hello, and thank you for returning my call. I'm calling in regards to one of your students, Robert Ryner. I wonder if you have a minute to talk to me about how he is doing." I knew I would need more than a minute but at least I would be able to share with her my immediate concerns.

As I listened to her I really wasn't surprised to hear that nothing had changed. It was as though I was reliving the previous year. The cruelty was still there, the home life the same. I learned she had talked to Mr. Peller and she herself was now seeing Robert exhibit the behavior that she had been warned about.

On a long shot, I called Dr. Halt to talk with her about Robert and what I had learned from the mother in addition to what had previously taken place at the end of the last school year. I also shared with her my research on children who have an incarcerated parent and the impact on their educations. We talked about Robert seeing his father going in and out of jail and how his father abused his mother. Then she made a comment I neither expected nor wanted to hear: "You do realize that research shows there is a genetic disposition for this child to end up like his father," she commented. Thus began a conversation from which we both learned.

The doctor began, "I had no idea that any of the things you shared with me ever happened. The mother never shared this with me; in fact, she missed last Thursday's session." Her voice could not contain her surprise at what she *didn't* know was happening in their lives. I felt terrible that the school's information about Robert had not reached the doctor, yet we had no idea that Robert's mother had sought outside counseling.

Still, there was so much I wanted to know; I needed to understand what was happening, so I pressed on. "Does Robert talk with you in the office? He never talks to us here at school. Do you ever see or talk about his father?" I had so many questions.

She confided, "The father is not in the picture and we haven't talked about him. Not only does he talk, but also while he is in my office he makes gestures that he wants to hurt his mother. He makes it clear that he doesn't like his mother and is embarrassed to be around her; he simply cannot contain himself. She never follows through with the visits. But I must say that she is a kind and sweet person, mentally challenged, but she doesn't lie. I don't believe he should maintain placement with his mother and in light of the recent things you shared with me, he should be removed from her and she can see him on the weekends." Dr. Halt's voice could not hide what she was feeling.

"Dr. Halt, he is so angry, I do believe that one day he will kill his mother."

"Well, unfortunately," she replied, "research does show that chronically criminal biological parents are likely to produce criminal sons."

Her words resounded in my ears with a deafening echo.

Can the sins of a father ever be overcome?

Was I kidding myself that a difference could be made?

Through the Eyes of Blue

POLICE OFFICER MIKE JAMES'S beat for the last two years has been in the most crime infested, poverty-stricken part of Rochester, New York. His experience in Rochester is not much different from the police work he did in Florida the previous eight years. Spending a decade working in crime-ridden areas can harden a man and his outlook on life, but Officer James has managed to retain his desire to make a difference in the lives of those he sees on a daily basis.

I had decided that, as a closing chapter to this book, it would be interesting and valuable to hear from someone on the front line of the fight against crime. Every day, Officer James comes up against situations in which children witness horrendous criminal acts, as well as their consequences under the law. During the ride along, his compassion and understanding for the children was evident. We scheduled a time and met on a Sunday afternoon at the police station before he started his shift, and I began by asking Officer James how he felt about the children on his beat who had to witness shocking events on a daily basis. It was clearly an issue that touched a nerve:

"I think that it's really detrimental to the kids to see the actual arrest," Officer James insisted. "Too many times, police officers respond to a call where there is family violence or parents dealing drugs, which calls for us to legally make an arrest and you're found doing it in front of the kids. I try to minimize that; I don't want the kids to form an opinion at such an early age that the police are bad or the police are the cause of the parents' problem or the police are the cause of their parents going to jail. The children are too young to understand that mommy and daddy have consequences for their actions. These kids, at such a young age, are forming opinions every time they're exposed to an arrest. Every time they see mom or dad get taken away in handcuffs, in a police car, they're forming negative opinions more times than not. These kids start to cry, clinging on to mom and dad, 'don't take my parents to jail.' Again, here we are, the authority figure, standing there in uniform, taking their role model, if you will, off to jail in handcuffs in the backseat of a police car.

"It really does a number on them mentally, even if it's not necessarily seen at that moment. Later down the road, there is an underlying basis for their actions or their negativity towards law enforcement or authority altogether. I'm not sure how I would have reacted as a child if my father was getting arrested. If it turns into a push and shove match, or, if you have to use force on the parent in front of the kid, it makes it 10 times worse. The kids look up to their parents and see them not only arrested but at times thrown on the ground, sprayed with pepper spray or even hit. Every time a kid

witnesses an arrest it just really impacts them in a negative way; they carry that with them right into their
adulthood. That's a lot of what we see in kids acting out
later in life. From the initial contact with police, they
are very negative, very rude, very disrespectful to law
enforcement officers and even authority figures.

"Last week we saw a black Honda go racing north-
bound. You could hear the engine revving. We saw it go
by and all of a sudden it makes this incredible U-turn
at full speed in the middle of the roadway. It then
speeds off in the other direction, so we turn around
and it takes us a few blocks to catch up to it because of
the speed he was running. We pull the car over and
there's a male and female in the car, with two kids in
the backseat. Neither of the kids was secured in their
child seats. This guy is driving with a complete lack of
concern for his own safety, much less the kids. So when
we stopped him, he doesn't have a license. When we
looked in the back seat we noticed they must have just
picked up dinner; the kids were eating. From what we
understood initially, mom and dad were having an
argument and it was his way of getting his frustration
out. He was making a turn to go home because the
mother of his children was throwing a fit and demanding to be taken home. He was just going to get her
there fast! He just totally didn't think about his kids."

"We took him out of the car and didn't handcuff
him in front of the kids since he was being respectful of
the situation. We took him to the police car to ID him
since he didn't have any identification on him. We had
him sit in our police car, unhandcuffed at the time
because it was a low level offense. We asked the female
what his name was and she gave us his correct name so

we sat back in the police car with this gentleman and asked him what his name was; he proceeded to lie to us. So I let him go on just long enough to make him understand that now he's committing a crime by falsely identifying himself as another person. Now he's committed a misdemeanor and that's an additional charge to whatever else he's hiding. He insists that it's his real name and I give him one final chance to come clean. 'If you come clean this very second, I'm not going to charge you with an additional crime. Just stop playing games with me.' So he finally does tell us what his real name is. He told us he's lying because he's got a warrant for his arrest, he's also got a suspended driver's license and he's pending court appearance for driving.

"So we go through all that and we have to arrest him because now, he's got a warrant for his arrest and the traffic charges so we're taking him downtown. My partner goes up and tells the women she can come back to the car because he wants to talk to her. So when she comes back, of course the kids jump out of the car and follow their mother. Now he's in the backseat of our police car, he starts calling his one son, 'Hey, poppy, you know, don't worry.' He's laughing, hamming it up with his kids. The two little boys around five and younger weren't in tears but they were very curious. Initially, he wasn't handcuffed but once we determined he was going to jail, we handcuffed him while he sat in the backseat. So, now the kids have gone up to the car, seen him, he's joking with them, they're wondering what's going on. He's trying to tell them, 'Oh, I've got some business to take care of.' The boys walked away and then came back a few minutes later.

"Now they're looking through the window at him with his hands cuffed behind his back. They know the handcuffs are on and here's dad in the police car. I felt that they were just wondering 'What's going on here? Why is my dad in the back of the police car? Why is my dad in handcuffs?' I could see the kids were initially happy to talk to him while he was in the backseat, but on that second approach, it was like the wind was taken out of them. They looked at us and looked at him and looked at mom. I think it's a situation they were uncomfortable with and there wasn't time to stand around and talk to the boys and explain to them what had happened.

"I was a police officer in Florida before I came here. I was there long enough to see kids, when I first got hired, especially in very run-down neighborhoods, very economically challenged families, no money, their sole income basis is drug money. The kids that were eight, nine years old, when I first came on, and then as I left eight years later, they were adults being arrested. One young man, between eight and 10, came up to the police car and said, 'Take me to jail.' I said, come on, man, we don't want to take you to jail. I tapped him on the head. 'We're not going to take you to jail.' He said, 'Well, my daddy's in jail, I got to go to jail.' It floored me! What a shame for him to think that progression in life means that as he becomes older, or as he comes of age he will go to jail just like his father. We didn't get into an in-depth conversation but I told him, 'you never want to go to jail' and he insisted, 'Well, my daddy's in jail. It ain't that bad in jail. You know, you got a place to sleep, you got food.' Somewhere along the way, someone has told this young man it's okay to be arrested.

He's a young black child; he lives in a predominately black neighborhood and sees police officers arresting black people all the time. It's ingrained in his mind, that's what's going to happen to him when he grows up—he's the next guy to go to jail. Every situation is different and each time I go on a call and the situation sounds the same, it is still different than the last one. But just maybe, one of these times, something's going to soak in. Someone's going to get the picture, take one of your suggestions, run with it and make a change in their life and you've had a positive impact.

"It's an endless cycle; you look at these kids that you deal with—white, black, Hispanic—it really goes across all lines, it's not just a certain race segment. You deal with all cross-sections of the community and it's difficult. It's a shame. I don't know what you can do to fix it. It's been like this for decades. What's going to happen in the next 20 years or 30 years in some of these neighborhoods? It seems to be getting progressively worse. The statistics are showing. You know more crime, more prisons, and more problems—an endless cycle."

The account of Officer James's experience is distressingly repeated and presented to us through data and statistics reported by the Bureau of Justice Statistics Special Report, Incarcerated Parents and Their Children. The report revealed that of the nation's 72.3 million minor children in 1999, 2.1 percent had a parent in state or federal prison. Black children were nine times more likely to have a parent in prison than white children. Hispanic children were three times as likely as white children to have an inmate parent. At year end in 1999 an estimated 1,372,700 minors had a father in state or federal prison, while another 126,100 children had a mother in prison. Since 1990 the number of all female prisoners has grown faster than that of male prisoners. As a result, the number of children with a mother in prison has nearly doubled since 1991, while the number of children with a father in prison grew by 58 percent during this period.

After listening to Officer James's story, I asked and received permission to ride with him during his shift, in order to witness first hand why the cycle has been impenetrable. What I witnessed left me feeling extremely anguished, yet with a deeper resolve that we must begin the journey to foster change among children with parents in prison.

The houses in the neighborhoods we drove through were boarded up and abandoned, many with broken windows. Filth and debris lined many of the homes and streets, weeds and overgrown grass were the norm. Many homes had their windows and doors covered with prison-like metal bars—their occupants, prisoners in their own homes. Storefronts were covered with metal mesh and padlocks; at first glance it was hard to tell if they were open. Only the men standing outside gave any hint that the stores were still in business. The weather was sultry and many of the people were sitting outside on their porches while children played in driveways and streets. Young girls with babies in their arms watched as we drove by. A closer look revealed they themselves were children, holding children. As we went to several calls with sirens and lights flashing most people didn't even bother to look—it was simply a common occurrence.

Domestic violence topped most of the calls and this particular call and the scene were very much the same. We arrived to see a mother screaming at the top of her lungs at the man in the car who was parked in her driveway. Her rage rose as we got out of the cruiser and approached her. "I can't believe that fucker called the police on me," she kept repeating over and over as she was pounding on the car. It was apparent that she was drunk from her staggering walk and slurred speech. There were two other men observing; each had a bottle of whiskey in a brown bag. Everyone was drunk.

One of the men, her boyfriend, kept yelling at her, "Bitch! You drunk. Shut the fuck up!" All the while, a young child watched and listened. The man in the car was very large, weighing more than 300 pounds, with a deep voice like James Earl Jones. He was one of the few people questioned over the course of the evening who didn't start the conversation with the word "fuck."

In the midst of it all, he remained calm. He was the father of both the children, a little seven-year-old the size of a four-year-old, and a nine-year-old in the back seat of the SUV. We didn't see the older child in the car until a closer look revealed him in the backseat where he was crouching down on the floor. The little one was running around the outside of the car peeking in through the open doors at his brother in the back seat while listening to the screaming and yelling. He ran into me on his way to the other side of the car still trying to get into the car to be with his brother and father. What a beautiful child! His dark hair in braids, his shorts two sizes too big and looking like long pants, no shirt, and pure white sneakers with no shoe laces; I suspected they were brand new. His eyes, as he looked up at me, were beautiful, piercing eyes that captured my heart.

Through the course of the screaming and yelling we learned that the older boy lived with his father while the younger child lived with his mother. The mother kept yelling at us that she and the children's father do this "fuckin' shit" all the time. Her rage continued as she screamed about the police being there and that she was capable of handling things. I learned that at one point or another they had all been arrested for disorderly conduct, domestic violence, drugs and other offenses. They had all spent time in jail. Finally, one of the men took the young child into the house. As the raging continued on, I could see the little child looking over the rail of the second-story porch. My words could never describe the innocence, fear and despair that I saw in his face. His mother wasn't arrested today, his father drove off with his older brother, and the police and I waved at the child as we left the drunken scene. The child didn't wave back; his eyes only followed us as we drove away. The officer didn't arrest her today, so tonight the child would have his mother home with him—on another day the story may have a very different ending.

Soon, a call came through the radio about a fight with crowds gathering and a child who had been hit by a brick. We arrived at the scene to see a group of 50 or more black males and females yelling and screaming at each other using the "F" word as though it were a pronoun. There were dozens of police cars and officers already on the scene talking to witnesses. A car was off to the side of the street with a smashed-in back window. Two children were in an ambulance near by.

Through the course of Officer James's investigation, the screaming was deafening. We learned that the driver of the car pulled over to the side of the street, jumped out of his car and started pounding on the female walking along the curb. It seems that hitting females is all in a day's work in this environment, since just about every call that we went on had some form of violence.

"When members of her family saw him beating her up," Officer James informed me after he conducted a brief investigation, "they came to her aid. One threw a brick through the back window while another was beating the man and his car with a stick"

As the crowd grew so did the number of police. People were everywhere, watching and listening. My first thought was to look for the child. When we arrived at the ambulance the children were splattered with blood, but after being checked out by the ambulance crew it was determined that the blood wasn't theirs. The woman who threw the brick in her rage of anger and defense of her family member never realized that two children were in the backseat of the car. The 10-month-old was only spared by the height of the car seat that protected him from the brick, and the four-year-old was simply fortunate that day. Their father was arrested as were several others, and while the children heard the screaming and watched the arrests from the ambulance, they clung to their mother.

Throughout the drive with Officer James, it never failed that when we arrived at the scene, the children always ran to the police officer and would call out, 'Hello, Mr. Policeman,' while tugging at his pants—unlike the adults who immediately began screaming their stories to him with some form of the adjective "fuck" in every other word. In the midst of the chaos and ear-piercing explanations of what happened, intermixed with swearing at each other and at the police, there were always little children watching, looking and listening—sadness in their eyes and tears streaming down their dirty little faces.

It was deja vu each time we arrived at a scene; for Officer James, it seemed to be an endless cycle. Over and over, year after year, he witnessed the same horrific situations. As I listened to him speak about the years that brought no change to the cycle and watched the heartbreaking reactions of the children during my ride with him, I kept thinking how prison begets prison and how poverty begets poverty. William Shakespeare said it best in *King Henry the Sixth* when he wrote, "Having nothing and nothing can he lose."

Children are especially vulnerable to being traumatized by violence because they feel helpless to prevent it. When an adult is out of control, there is very little a child can do to bring order to the situation. Violence in the home is a tremendous source of anxiety for children. Seeing a stranger assaulted is alarming for a child, but seeing a parent or relative assaulted is devastating.

Children learn how to behave from the actions they see in their parental role models. Aggressive and violent behavior is learned at an early age. It begins in the family, expands through the culture of the community and larger society in which the child grows and matures, and then comes full circle where it is reinforced or discouraged by the family.

If we, as a society, do not begin to pay attention to the needs of children with parents in prison, this cycle of criminal behavior will continue to expand and the crimes committed will multiply. We must stop ignoring this critical problem and address it head-on, one child at a time.

The Research

"In this sad world of ours, sorrow comes to all; and, to the young, it comes with bitterest agony, because it takes them unawares. The older have learned to expect it."
—*Abraham Lincoln*

The poignant stories you have just read expose the truths and experiences of the 2.3 million children with parents in prison. In the United States, the rate at which adults are being incarcerated, and the children they leave behind, reflect our own social negligence.

In *Utopia,* Sir Thomas More writes, "For if you suffer your people to be ill-educated, and their manners to be corrupted from their infancy, and then punish them for those crimes to which their first education disposed them, what else is to be concluded from this, but that you first make thieves and then punish them?"

More wrote in the 15th century and Lincoln in the 18th century. Yet their words still speak to us now, and we must adhere to their truths if we are to solve the problem of our growing prison population and the children who are its innocent victims.

Neil Bernstein's essay, *A Sentence of Their Own,* includes the following: "Johnston, of the Center for Children of

Incarcerated Parents, recognizes that the public has little compassion for offenders, or even for their children. 'One of the basic motivations of this society is retribution,' she says. We need to make ourselves feel better by hurting people who have done something wrong. 'But in the long run,' she points out, the urge for retribution 'ends up costing us.' The heaviest cost is being carried by the generation of children growing up in the shadow of the prison."

The costs of imprisonment are devastating and the overview of statistics distressing. The Child Welfare League of America, Federal Resource Center for Children of Prisoners provides the most comprehensive and most quoted statistics on the subject. The CWLA reports the following:

> According to the Bureau of Justice Statistics, they estimate that 2.3 million children are affected by the 1.1 million parents incarcerated in prisons or jails, up from 500,000 children in 1991. More than 7 million children have a parent under some form of correctional supervision. With the nation's annual average incarcerated population growing at a rate of 3.8 percent annually, the number of children with parents in prison will likely continue to increase. Fifty-eight percent of children are younger than 10. Their average age is eight. Approximately 10 percent of the children of female prisoners and 2 percent of the children of male prisoners are in a foster home or institution.

With regards to men in prison, the Child Welfare League notes:

> By midyear 2002, more than 1.8 million men were incarcerated in state and federal prisons and local jails. Since 1995, the number of male inmates has increased at an average annual rate of 3.6 percent. Their family background and characteristics include the following: The typical male inmate grew up in a single-parent home and has at least one family member who has been incarcerated. More than one-third has experienced the incarceration of an immediate family member. One in seven was raised by relatives; 17 percent spent time in out-of-home care. Most male offenders have limited education and poor employment skills. At the time of their arrest, 90 percent had an income below $25,000, and 69 percent had an income below poverty level. Approximately 55 percent of incarcerated men are fathers of children younger than 18. Thirty-two percent have two or more children under the age of 18. Fifty-seven percent of fathers reported never having visits from their children.

The Child Welfare League's statistics on women in prison state the following:

> At the end of 2002, 96,099 women were under the jurisdiction of state or federal correctional authorities, an increase of 1.9 percent from 2001, compared with a 1.4 percent increase of men. Since 1995, the number of women inmates has

grown at an average annual rate of 5.4 percent, higher than the 3.6 percent average increase for male inmates. The family characteristics and background of women in prison include the following: The typical female offender comes from a single-parent home in which other family members have been incarcerated. One in five has lived in a family foster home or group care facility while growing up. Nearly six in 10 in state prisons report having experienced physical or sexual abuse in the past. Most women in prison have limited education and poor employment skills; less than half completed high school. Of the incarcerated mothers, 75 percent of incarcerated women are mothers, and two-thirds have children under the age of 18. Seventy-two percent of women prisoners with children under age 18 lived with those children before entering prison. Six percent of women entering prison are pregnant. From 1990 to 2000, the number of mothers in prison grew 87 percent, while fathers increased by 61 percent. Fifty-four percent of mothers in state prisons said they never had visits from their children.

According to the Independent Television Service's *When the Bough Breaks—Mothers in Prison:*

Further studies show that six percent of women are pregnant when they enter prison, yet most states make no special arrangements for the care of newborns. Pregnant inmates are often required to be shackled while giving birth, and after delivery, mothers and babies are sometimes separated within hours. The infant is then sent to live with a family member or is placed in the foster care system.

Too little attention has been paid to the plights of children with incarcerated parents and therefore too little is known about how to assist them. This point is driven home in Cynthia Seymour and Creasie Finney Harriston's *Children with Parents in Prison*. "There is no procedure or policy established to inquire about dependent children when a mother is arrested," the authors write. "Only if the child enters the social service system are child welfare workers legally mandated to facilitate parent-child visits when such visits are not detrimental to the child. Visiting can decrease the stress of separation, enable children to maintain relationships with parents, and increase the likelihood of successful reunification."

Elizabeth Johnson and Jane Waldfogel address the concerns of where children live when parents are incarcerated in addition to the affects these placements have on the children in *Where Children Live When Parents Are Incarcerated*:

The majority (77 percent) of children whose fathers are incarcerated remain or go to live with their mothers, while about five percent live with a grandparent or relative. When mothers are incarcerated, children most often live with grandparents or other relatives. Only 17 percent live with their fathers. Children of incarcerated mothers are also more likely to be placed in a foster home—six percent compared with 1 percent of incarcerated fathers' children.

Denise Johnston and Michael Carlin recently wrote about another impact of incarceration in *When Incarcerated Parents Lose Contact with Their Children*. "It is becoming increasingly common for incarcerated parents to lose contact with their children," they state, "and/or knowledge of their whereabouts, during their time in jail and/or prison. The Center for Children of Incarcerated Parents receives more than 400 letters per year from prisoners who cannot find their children."

Among both State and Federal prisoners with minor children, blacks comprised the largest racial/ethnic group. In state prisons, 49 percent of parents were black, 29 percent white, and 19 percent Hispanic (Mumola). The statistics are alarming and according to Antoine Garibaldi's *Educating and Motivating African American Males to Succeed*, one of the most actively discussed, and sometimes vigorously debated issues since the late 1980s has been the declining social, economic, and educational status of young African American males in our society. The negative indicators that describe a substantial share of this group's depressing condition in unemployment statistics, homicidal rates (as both victims and perpetrators), their overwhelmingly disproportionate representation in the criminal justice system, as well as their last-place ranking on many measures of educational performance and attainment have become so commonplace that it has caused many to view the majority of these young men's future as hopeless and impossible to salvage. Garibaldi further states, "Even if one doubts that a 'crisis' truly exists or questions whether African American males may one day become an 'endangered species,' few systematic solutions have been offered to address realistically the problems that at least one-third of young black men experience."

In a paper presented at the Annual Meeting of the American Society of Criminology, Michelle Evans and John Rogers pointed out that, "Whether the arrestee is the primary caretaker, a source of financial and emotional support for the minor child or is simply a member of the child's family, arrest and incarceration itself have been shown to have a negative impact on the health and welfare of the child." Their research concluded that "even interpreted conservatively, these findings indicate a need for further research as well as specific intervention and public policy strategies addressing criminal justice involvement as a family event."

Tori De Angelis reaffirms the devastating impact of parental incarceration in her essay *Punishment of Innocents: Children of Parents Behind Bars*, in which she explains: "Most of these youngsters deal with a combination of inadequate parenting and shame at having a parent in prison, as well as poverty. Many drop out of school and many are prey to sexual and physical abuse, neglect, and substance abuse. Worse, most of these youngsters never receive help, and consequently, many become offenders themselves. Research on, and programs for, these children are scarce."

John Hagan writes of the collateral damage in his paper, The *Next Generation: Children of Prisoners:*

A father or mother's imprisonment can be the final blow to an already weakened family structure. The fact that a large number of parents are being imprisoned implies that there is a neglected class of young people whose lives are disrupted as well as damaged by their separation from imprisoned mothers and fathers. As a family disintegrates, children experience prolonged and intensified periods of instability and uncertainty. These children's problems are the largely hidden and uncalculated cost of imprisonment. Prior studies indicate that very little is actually known about the causal role that the penal sanctioning of parents plays in children's lives, alone or in combination with other experiences and events in the lives of these children. There is an urgent need for new and better-designed studies focused on the children of incarcerated parents.

I have experienced first-hand the range of negative outcomes and emotional and psychological scarring of the children and their families. In *Prisoners Once Removed: The Children and Families of Prisoners*, Michelle Waul and Jeremy Travis state, "A few studies have found that children of incarcerated parents are more likely to exhibit low self-esteem, depression, emotional withdrawal from friends and family, and inappropriate or disruptive behavior at home and in school. In addition, some evidence suggests that children of incarcerated parents are at high risk for future delinquency and/or criminal behavior."

I've witnessed these same emotions and behaviors in the children I studied for this book. One student in particular experienced such significant depression and behavioral difficulties both at home and school that her pediatrician decided to place her on Paxil. The

FDA Talk Paper's research on the medication reveals the following:

> The FDA has completed a new analysis of pediatric suicidality (suicidal thoughts and actions) data submitted to the agency and will be posting its analysis on its web site. The FDA has been closely reviewing the results of antidepressant studies in children since June 2003, after an initial report on studies with paroxetine (Paxil) appeared to suggest an increased risk of suicidal thoughts and actions in children given Paxil, compared to those given placebo. Later reports on studies of other drugs supported the possibility of an increased risk of suicidality, thoughts and actions in children taking these drugs. There were no suicides in any of the trials.

The needs of the child and the knowledge we now have regarding Paxil have the school closely monitoring her behavior. We have become advocates for the child by working to assure that the increased risks of suicidal thoughts and actions do not turn this child into a statistic.

According to the San Francisco Partnership for Incarcerated Parents, a coalition of social service providers, little is known about what becomes of children when their parents are imprisoned. There is no requirement that the various institutions charged with dealing with offenders— the police, courts, jails and prisons, probation departments—inquire about children's existence. Seymour and Hairston state that, "[A]lthough the number of children affected by parental incarceration can be estimated, the true scope of the problem is uncertain because few reliable statistics exist. For the most part, law enforcement does not gather information about the children of arrested adults and correctional institutions do not ask prisoners for specific information about their children. Because there is no specific agency or system charged with collecting data about this population, it is unclear how many children are affected, who they are, or where they live."

The Prison Policy Initiative conducts research and advocacy on incarceration policies. Their work starts with the following idea:

> The racial, gender and economic disparities between the prison population and the larger society represent the grounds for a democratic catastrophe. Their conception of prison reform is based not solely in opposing a rising rate of incarceration, but in evolving to a better way of addressing social problems than warehousing our citizens in cages. Their statistics send a cry for change: The percent of state prisoner parents incarcerated 100–500 miles from their last place of residence was 51.2 percent. The percent of federal prisoner parents incarcerated more than 100 miles from their last place of residence is 84.0 percent. The percent of prisoners who had no visits in their final year of prison and were arrested in their first year on parole was 50 percent. In comparison to the percent of prisoners who had three visits in their final year of prison who were arrested in their first year on parole was 30 percent."

The stories in this book give a descriptive view of the children and families attached to a parent in prison. The emotional and behavioral consequences, the lack of contact, the geographic distance that separates the child from the adult, the exposure to adult content, the shame, and, in many cases, the treatment of children as though *they* have committed a crime. There is a definite need for the current system to be analyzed as to its effectiveness; the statistics call for change.

There are agencies that have begun to look at the problem as the alarming rates are beginning to command attention. The U.S. Department of Justice, Federal Bureau of Prisons is an agency that provides the most comprehensive and most quoted statistics on the subject:

According to the U.S. Department of Justice, Federal Bureau of Prisons (2004) beginning in 1986, the United States Congressional appropriations conference reports for the Bureau included recommended parenting program funding levels. Initially, funding was provided at four female institutions and subsequently at all female institutions and at least one male institution in each region. Conferences reports also identified appropriate visiting room space, parent education, social service outreach, and community-based service providers as desirable parenting program characteristics. This Program Statement expands such programs to all institutions.

Program Objectives. The expected results of this program are:

A) Positive relationships, family values, and mutual support and nurturing, which may be sustained after release, will be promoted and reinforced among inmates and their spouses and children.

B) Each inmate will have opportunities to counteract negative family consequences resulting from his/her incarceration.

C) The institutional social environment will be improved through opportunities for inmates to maintain positive and sustaining contracts with their families.

D) Social services and community-based organizations will be included in parenting programs whenever possible.

Interestingly, this report (dated January 20, 1995) also states that standards in all institutions have been met.

According to the National Institute of Corrections, Services for Families of Prison Inmates, "A variety of studies have found that increased contact between inmates and their families can contribute to an inmate's re-integration into the community after release. Institutional programming and visitations can encourage healthier family relationships, further developing a critical element in the offender's post-release support system."

The National Institute of Corrections, U.S. Department of Justice identified the following as a starting point for understanding the complex issue of having a parent incarcerated as well as understanding the issue from a child's point of view:

Children of Incarcerated Parents: A Bill of Rights: to be kept safe and informed at the time of my parents arrest; to be heard when decisions are made about me; to be considered when decisions are made about my parent; to be well cared for in my parents absence; to speak with, see, and touch my parent; to be supported as I struggle with my parents incarceration; not to be judged, blamed, or labeled because of my parents incarceration; and to a lifelong relationship with my parents.

In January of 2003, President George W. Bush delivered his State of the Union address. His concern for the children of parents in prison was apparent:

Tonight I ask Congress and the American people to focus the spirit of service and the resources of government on the needs of some of our most vulnerable citizens—boys and girls trying to grow up without guidance and attention, and children who have to go through a prison gate to be hugged by their mom or dad. I propose a $450-million initiative to bring mentors to more than a million disadvantaged junior high students and children of prisoners. Government will support the training and recruiting of mentors; yet it is the men and women of America who will fill the need. One mentor, one person can change a life forever. And I urge you to be that one person.

In a press release by the Office of Minority Health Resource Center on August 3, 2004, President Bush announced $45.6 million dollars in grants to provide mentors to children of prisoners. "Mentors are the heroes who provide a trusting relationship with a child or youth in need," HHS Secretary Tommy G. Thompson said, "We know that youth outcomes can be improved with the help of a mentor. Today's grants will give young Americans the hope and guidance they need to grow up to be successful, healthy adults."

The press release went on to say:

The research had found that significant physical absence of a parent has profound effects on child development. Children of incarcerated parents are seven times more likely to become involved in the juvenile and adult criminal justice systems. Parental arrest and confinement often leads to stress, trauma, stigmatization and separation problems for children. These problems may be compounded by existing poverty, violence, substance abuse, high-crime environments, child abuse and neglect, multiple caregivers and/or prior separations. The need for mentors and committed adults was at the foundation for the grant monies.

It is this author's opinion that much of the research on children with parents in prison is limited. There is no federal policy or one organization charged with collecting the data necessary to track those left behind when a parent is imprisoned. To date, there have been no longitudinal studies on the children; there are no comprehensive assessments on this population.

Furthermore, the literature on the subject is minimal and dated. The variables are exhaustive and the need for a widespread study imperative. The subject is one of despair; however, pockets of society within several organizations are pioneering programs for these children. These organizations work with compassion and understanding, and they are accomplishing their goals one child at a time.

Bibliography

Abraham Lincoln Online, Speeches & Writings. Retrieved November 2, 2004, from http://showcase.netins.net/web/creative/lincoln/speeches/mccull.htm

Bernstein, Neil. (*Left Behind: Tens of Thousands of Children Have a Parent Behind Bars. What Are the Social Costs of Their Loss?* Retrieved October 22, 2004, from A Sentence of Their Own: Essays — Left Behind Web site: http://www.asentenceoftheirown.com? Essays%20-%20 Left%20Behind.html

Bronowski, Jacob. *The Ascent of Man.* Boston: Brown and Company, 1973.

Bush, George. W., *State of the Union Address.* 2003. Retrieved October 19, 2004, from http://www.whitehouse.gov/news/releases/2003/01/20030128-19.html

Chapman, A.H. *The Games Children Play.* New York: G.P. Putnam's Sons, 1971.

Child Welfare League of America, Federal Resource Center of Children of Prisoners Policy, Program, and

Practice Issues. Retrieved July 24, 2004, from Child Welfare League of America Web site: http://www. cwla.org/programs/incarcerated/cop_factsheet.htm

DeAngelis, Tori. *Punishment of Innocents: Children of Parents Behind Bars. 2001.* Retrieved July 7, 2004, from Monitor on Psychology Web site: http://www.apa.org/ monitor/may01/punish.html

Durosimni, Brenda. M.P.A. *When Children Witness Violence.* Retrieved August 14, 2004, from, University of Nevada, Reno, Cooperative Extension: http://www. unce.unr.edu/publications/FS97/FS9743.htm

Evans, Michelle, B., Rogers, John, D. *The Impact of Substance Use and Incarceration on Childcare.* 2003. Public Research Institute, San Francisco State University, Paper Presentation.

FDA Talk Paper. FDA Updates Its Review of Antidepressant Drugs in Children. Retrieved August 23, 2004, from http://www.fda.gov/bbs/topics/ANSWERS? 2004/ANS01302.html

Federal Bureau of Prisons. *Parenting Program Standards.* 1995. Retrieved September 9, 2004, from Federal Bureau of Prisons Web site: http://www.bop.gov/ipapg. ipaover.html

Garibaldi, Antoine, M. *Educating and Motivating African American Males to Succeed.* Journal of Negro Education, Vol. 61, No. 1, 1992.

Ginnott, Haim G. *Between Parents and Child*. New York: MacMillan, 1965.

Hagan, John. *The Next Generation: Children of Prisoners.* 2001. Retrieved May 1, 2001, from: http://www.doc.state.ok.us/DOCS/OCJRC/Ocjrc96/Ocjrc19.htm

Independent Television Service: *When the Bough Breaks — Mothers in Prison*. Retrieved October 22, 2004, from http://www.itvs.org/whentheboughbreaks/mothers. htms

Johnston, Denise, J., & Carlin, Michael. *When Incarcerated Parents Lose Contact with Their Children*. CCIP Journal, Vol. 6, Number 1, 2004. Retrieved October 22, 2004, from The Center of Children of Incarcerated Parents. Web site: http://www.e.ccip.org/journal.html

Johnson, Elizabeth, I., & Waldfogel, Jane. *Where Children Live When Parents Are Incarcerated*. 2003. Retrieved October 22, 2004, from The Joint Center for Poverty Research Web site: http://www.jcpr.org/policy-briefs/vol5 numb4.html

Lewis, Thomas. *The Fragile Species*. New York: Charles Scribner's Sons, 1992.

More, Sir Thomas. *Utopia*. 1516. [Electronic version]. Retrieved October 25, 2004, from http://www.constitu-tion.org/index.shtml

Mumola, Christopher, J. Bureau of Justice Statistics Special Report: *Incarcerated Parents and Their Children*. 2000. Retrieved November 30, 2001 from U.S. Department of

Justice Bureau of Justice Statistics Web site: http://www.ojp.usdoj.gov/bjs/crimoff.htm

National Institute of Correction. *Services for Families of Prison Inmates*. 2002. Retrieved October 22, 2004, from http://www.nicic.org/Library/018895

Office of Minority Health Resource Center. *President Announces Mentoring Grants for Children of Prisoners*. 2004. Retrieved October 22, 2004, from Web site: http://www.omhrc.gov/omhrc/pressreleases/2004press0803.htm

Prison Policy Initiative. Retrieved October 22, 2004, from http://www.prisonpolicy.org/index.shtml

Salk, Lee. *What Every Child Would Like His Parents to Know*. New York: David McKay Company, Inc., 1972.

San Francisco Partnership for Incarcerated Parents. *Children of Incarcerated Parents: A Bill of Rights*. 2003.

Seymour, Cynthia, Harriston, Creasie Finney. *Children with Parents in Prison*. Child Welfare League of America, Inc. Transaction Publishers: 2001.

Steinbeck, John. *East of Eden*. New York: Biking Press, Inc., 1952.

Waul, Michelle, Travis, Jeremy. *Prisoners Once Removed: The Children and Families of Prisoners*. 2004. The Urban Institute [Electronic Version]. Retrieved October 19, 2004, from Web site: http://www.urban.org/pubs/prisoners/chapter1.html

Resources

Active Parenting Publishers
http://www.activeparenting.com
APP delivers quality education programs for parents, children and teachers to schools, hospitals, social services organizations, churches, and the corporate market. The Active Parenting model is heavily based upon the theories of Alfred Adler and Rudolf Dreikurs.

Administration for Children and Families
http://wwwacf.dhhs.gov
The Administration for Children and Families, within the Department of Health and Human Services is responsible for federal programs that promote the economic and social well-being of families, children, individuals, and communities.

Administration for Children and Families
http://www.ncfy.com/mcp-biblio.htm
This Web site features the "Mentoring Children of Prisoners Bibliography," which provides articles and links to sites dealing with issues surrounding children with parents in prison.

Alliance for Children and Families
http://wwwalliance1.org
The Alliance for Children and Families is a national membership association that provides effective resources and leadership to over 300 private, nonprofit child- and family-serving organizations in the United States and Canada.

American Library Association
http://www.ala.org
The American Library Association's mission is to promote the highest quality library and information services and public access to information. ALA offers professional services and publications to members and nonmembers.

Angel Tree Newsroom
http://www.demossnewspond.com
The only nationwide, year-round effort to reach out exclusively to children whose fathers or mothers are behind bars.

Bureau of Justice Statistics
http://www.ojp.usdoj.gov
A unit of the U.S. Department of Justice whose principal function is the compilation and analysis of data and the dissemination of information for statistical purposes.

Capitol City Publishers
http://capitolcitypublishers.com
Capitol City Publishers provide specialized news, information and analysis via several different channels,

including newsletters, executive reports, conferences, and the Internet.

Center of Children of Incarcerated Parents
http://www.e-ccip.org
The Center of Children of Incarcerated Parents' mission is the prevention of intergenerational crime and incarceration. Their goals are the production of high-quality documentation on and the development of model services for children of criminal offenders and their families.

Chicago Legal Aid to Incarcerated Mothers
http://www.c-l-a-I-m.org
CLAIM provides legal and educational services to the families of women prisoners, with the goal of maintaining family bonds through the period of incarceration.

Child Abuse Prevention Project
http://mchneighborhood.ichp.edu/capp/
CAPP provides a variety of services including in-home parent education, parent education groups, moms-in-prison groups, professional training, and consultation.

Child Welfare League of America
http://www.cwla.org
The first national organization devoted to protecting children and strengthening families. The League remains one of the largest organizations of its kind.

Children's Literacy Foundation
http://www.clifonline.org
CLiF is working with prison educators to encourage inmates to read with their children during visiting hours as well as foster a love of reading between parent and child.

Citizens United for Rehabilitation of Errants
http://www.curenational.org/
CURE, a national nonprofit, addresses crime reduction through reform of the criminal justice system itself. The organization promotes fair, human treatment of prisoners, seeks alternatives to incarceration where possible, and advocates abolition of capital punishment.

Directory of Programs Serving Families of Adult Offenders
http://www.fcnetwork.org/Dir98/dir98front.html
Provides resources on American and Canadian programs that assist the families of adult offenders, prepared by the Family and Corrections Network. Listings are organized by state, and include contact information and program descriptions.

Families with Loved Ones in Prison, Inc.
http://www.afn.org/~flip/
A nonprofit dedicated to maintaining ties between prisoners and their loved ones in order to counteract recidivism. The organization promotes humane treatment for those visiting prisoners.

Family and Corrections Network
http://wwwfcnetwork.org
An organization for and about families of prisoners. The organization offers information, training and technical assistance on children of prisoners, parenting programs for prisoners, prison visiting, incarcerated fathers and mothers, hospitality programs, keeping in touch, returning to the community, the impact of the justice system on families, and prison marriage. This site is the gateway to practice, policy and research on families of prisoners.

The Father Resource Network
http://www.father.com
The site's mission is to provide a network of referral and resource support services that help solve the problems and challenges associated with fatherhood today. The programs provide reliable services and powerful solutions to manage challenges and time-consuming tasks. The suite of forward-thinking educational services and solutions provide recipients with the help they need to improve their lives.

Journal of Extension
http://www.joe.org
The Journal of Extension is a peer-reviewed journal that seeks to expand and update the research and knowledge base for adult educators to improve their effectiveness.

◆

Legal Services for Prisoners with Children
http://prisonerswithchildren.org
LSPC advocates for the human rights and empowerment of incarcerated parents, children, family members and people at risk for incarceration. They respond to requests for information, trainings, technical assistance, litigation, community activism, and the development of more advocates. The focus is on women prisoners and their families, and the organization emphasizes that issues of race are central to any discussion of incarceration.

National Institute of Corrections
http://nicic.org
A center of correctional learning and experience. The institute advances and shapes effective correctional practice and public policy, and promotes corrections through collaboration and leadership and by providing assistance, information, education, and training.

National Service Resource Center
http://nationalserviceresources.org.
Resources relating to community service and volunteering.

Parents and Children Together, Inc.
http://www.fcnetwork.org/programs/pact.html
A nonprofit established in 1984, PACT strives to break the cycle of incarceration through preservation and fortification of the families of incarcerated individuals.

Prison Fellowship Newsroom
http://www.demossnewspond.com
Prison Fellowship provides ongoing support, recruitment, research, training, and resources to the more than 20,000 churches throughout America. It also works with thousands more individual volunteers, who are active in outreach to prison populations or inmate families. Programs of Prison Fellowship include outreach to prisoners, ex-prisoner transitional care, assistance to families and children of prisoners, and advocacy for criminal justice reform.

Prison Support Directory
http://prisonactivist.org/psd.htm
Provides information on organizations serving inmates and their families. Also includes resources about prison AIDS, advocacy organizations, parole and pre-release information, and legal matters.

Society of Clinical Psychology
http://www.apa.org
The Society of Clinical Psychology is based in Washington, D.C.

Therapeutic Resources
http://wwwtherapeuticresources.com
Provides easy-to-use, time-saving and effective educational products to assist in the development of life skills and personal growth.

Urban Institute
http://www.urban.org
In their own words, a "nonpartisan economic and social policy research organization."

Volunteers of America
http://volunteersofamerica.org
Provides outreach programs that deal with today's most pressing social needs. Volunteers of America helps youths at risk, the elderly, abused and neglected children, people with disabilities, homeless individuals, and many others.

Women Coping in Prison
http://curry.edschool.virginia.edu/prisonstudy/home.html
Resources on incarcerated women, including scientific studies and academic articles.

A Call to Action

Dear Reader:

According to the Child Welfare League of America's Federal Resource Center for Children of Prisoners, 2.3 million children are affected by the 1.1 million parents incarcerated in prisons or jails—up from 500,000 children in 1991. More than 7 million children have a parent under some form of correctional supervision.

With the nation's annual average incarcerated population growing at a rate of 3.8 percent annually, the number of children with parents in prison will undoubtedly continue to increase. Fifty-eight percent of these children are younger than 10 years old; their average age is eight. According to the American School Counselor Association, of the 72 million young children in this country, one child in 50 has a parent in prison.

To address the needs of these children and the impact the incarceration of parents has on children, I have created the "Loving Through Bars" organization. If you would like to help the children in this book and other children with parents in prison, please contact us at:

> Loving Through Bars
> Children with Parents in Prison
> P.O. Box 3615
> Erie, PA 16508
> lovingthroughbars@yahoo.com

Non Profit Corporation federal tax exemption filing is pending.

Sincerely,

Cynthia Martone
January 2005

Books Available
from Santa Monica Press

American Hydrant
by Sean Crane
176 pages $24.95

Blues for Bird
by Martin Gray
288 pages $16.95

The Book of Good Habits
*Simple and Creative Ways to
Enrich Your Life*
by Dirk Mathison
224 pages $9.95

The Butt Hello
*and other ways my cats
drive me crazy*
by Ted Meyer
96 pages $9.95

Childish Things
by Davis & Davis
96 pages $19.95

**Discovering the History of
Your House**
and Your Neighborhood
by Betsy J. Green
288 pages $14.95

The Dog Ate My Resumé
by Zack Arnstein and Larry
Arnstein
192 pages $11.95

Dogme Uncut
*Lars von Trier, Thomas Vinterberg
and the Gang That Took on
Hollywood*
by Jack Stevenson
312 pages $16.95

**Exotic Travel Destinations for
Families**
by Jennifer M. Nichols
and Bill Nichols
360 pages $16.95

Footsteps in the Fog
Alfred Hitchcock's San Francisco
by Jeff Kraft and
Aaron Leventhal
240 pages $24.95

**Free Stuff & Good Deals for
Folks over 50, 2nd Ed.**
by Linda Bowman
240 pages $12.95

**How to Find Your Family Roots
and Write Your Family History**
by William Latham and
Cindy Higgins
288 pages $14.95

How to Speak Shakespeare
by Cal Pritner and
Louis Colaianni
144 pages $16.95

**How to Win Lotteries,
Sweepstakes, and Contests in
the 21st Century, 2nd Edition**
by Steve "America's
Sweepstakes King" Ledoux
224 pages $14.95

**Jackson Pollock:
Memories Arrested in Space**
by Martin Gray
216 pages $14.95

James Dean Died Here
*The Locations of America's Pop
Culture Landmarks*
by Chris Epting
312 pages $16.95

The Keystone Kid
Tales of Early Hollywood
by Coy Watson, Jr.
312 pages $24.95

**The Largest U.S. Cities Named
after a Food**
by Brandt Maxwell
360 pages $16.95

Letter Writing Made Easy!
*Featuring Sample Letters for
Hundreds of Common Occasions*
by Margaret McCarthy
224 pages $12.95

**Letter Writing Made Easy!
Volume 2**
*Featuring More Sample Letters for
Hundreds of Common Occasions*
by Margaret McCarthy
224 pages $12.95

Life is Short. Eat Biscuits!
by Amy Jordan Smith
96 pages $9.95

Loving Through Bars
Children with Parents in Prison
by Cynthia Martone
208 pages $21.95

Marilyn Monroe Dyed Here
*More Locations of America's
Pop Culture Landmarks*
by Chris Epting
312 pages $16.95

Movie Star Homes
by Judy Artunian and
Mike Oldham
312 pages $16.95

Offbeat Museums
*The Collections and Curators of
America's Most Unusual Museums*
by Saul Rubin
240 pages $19.95

A Prayer for Burma
by Kenneth Wong
216 pages $14.95

Quack!
*Tales of Medical Fraud from the
Museum of Questionable Medical
Devices*
by Bob McCoy
240 pages $19.95

Redneck Haiku
by Mary K. Witte
112 pages $9.95

**School Sense: How to Help
Your Child Succeed in
Elementary School**
by Tiffani Chin, Ph.D.
408 pages $16.95

Silent Echoes
*Discovering Early Hollywood
Through
the Films of Buster Keaton*
by John Bengtson
240 pages $24.95

Tiki Road Trip
*A Guide to Tiki Culture in
North America*
by James Teitelbaum
288 pages $16.95

Order Form 1-800-784-9553

	Quantity	Amount
American Hydrant ($24.95)		
Blues for Bird (epic poem about Charlie Parker) ($16.95)		
The Book of Good Habits ($9.95)		
The Butt Hello . . . and Other Ways My Cats Drive Me Crazy ($9.95)		
Childish Things ($19.95)		
Discovering the History of Your House. . . ($14.95)		
The Dog Ate My Resumé ($11.95)		
Dogme Uncut ($16.95)		
Exotic Travel Destinations for Families ($16.95)		
Footsteps in the Fog: Alfred Hitchcock's San Francisco ($24.95)		
Free Stuff & Good Deals for Folks over 50, 2nd Ed. ($12.95)		
How to Find Your Family Roots . . . ($14.95)		
How to Speak Shakespeare ($16.95)		
How to Win Lotteries, Sweepstakes, and Contests . . . ($14.95)		
Jackson Pollock: Memories Arrested in Space ($14.95)		
James Dean Died Here: America's Pop Culture Landmarks ($16.95)		
The Keystone Kid: Tales of Early Hollywood ($24.95)		
The Largest U.S. Cities Named after a Food ($16.95)		
Letter Writing Made Easy! ($12.95)		
Letter Writing Made Easy! Volume 2 ($12.95)		
Life is Short. Eat Biscuits! ($9.95)		
Loving Through Bars ($21.95)		
Marilyn Monroe Dyed Here ($16.95)		
Movie Star Homes ($16.95)		
Offbeat Museums ($19.95)		
A Prayer for Burma ($14.95)		
Quack! Tales of Medical Fraud ($19.95)		
Redneck Haiku ($9.95)		
School Sense ($16.95)		
Silent Echoes: Early Hollywood Through Buster Keaton ($24.95)		
Tiki Road Trip ($16.95)		

	Subtotal	
	CA residents add 8.25% sales tax	

Shipping & Handling:
1 book $3.00
Each additional book is $ .50

Shipping and Handling (see left)

TOTAL

Name ————————————————————————————

Address ——————————————————————————

City ———————————————— State ——————— Zip ———————

❏ Visa ❏ MasterCard   Card No.: —————————————————————

Exp. Date ———————————— Signature ————————————

❏ Enclosed is my check or money order payable to:

Santa Monica Press LLC
P.O. Box 1076
Santa Monica, CA 90406
www.santamonicapress.com   1-800-784-9553